'I Can't Watch Anymore'

Author's Note

As this book was being sent off to print, news outlets worldwide reported that the Union Internationale de Pentathlon Moderne (UIPM) was set to drop the equestrian discipline from its programme. The ordeal suffered by the horse Saint Boy during the modern pentathlon equestrian event at the Tokyo Olympic Games, and the global outrage which followed, had sealed the deal. The UIPM could no longer afford to exploit horses as mere sports equipment if it wanted to survive as an Olympic sport. We were not able to wait for the final outcome, but whatever it is, the case of modern pentathlon has served to turn all eyes on the horses performing in the Olympics. The problems of welfare, fairness, and safety addressed in this book must be resolved, and the only way to do this now is to discontinue Equestrian from the Olympic Games.

'I Can't Watch ANYMORE'

The Case for Dropping Equestrian from the Olympic Games: An Open Letter to the International Olympic Committee

Julie Taylor

Published by Epona Media
Copenhagen, January 2022
www.epona.tv

ISBN 978-87-973543-0-8

Editing and typesetting by Ashwood Publishing,
Cradoc, Tasmania, Australia.
ashwoodpublishing.com.au

Cover photo by Crispin Parelius Johannessen
Cover design by Ashwood Publishing

Contents

Preface vii

1 **Equestrian: a sport for all?** 1
The myth of gender equality 1
Economic barriers to participation 2
More flags does not really mean more participation in equestrian events 5
Promoting grassroots take-up of equestrian sport? 8
Poverty-washing PR is demeaning and potentially harmful 12
Abuse of power in equestrian sport 16

2 **Animals in the Olympics are a liability, not an asset** 20
Animal exploitation and the Olympic brand 22
No evidence horses want to compete 24

3 **Modern horse sport does not represent tradition** 31
Traditional horsemanship and modern competition 32
Equestrian traditions and modern times 38

4 **Doping, cheating, and why equestrian sport can never be clean** 40
The normalisation of drugs that enhance performance 45
Clean or corrupt, international horse sport and welfare don't mix 52
Additional difficulties in avoiding prohibited substances in horses 60

5 **The stories of Anton and Never** 63
Removal of the ban on de-nerved horses in competition 65
Implications of allowing de-nerved horses in competition 71

6 **Equestrian rules are unenforceable** 74
A growing gap between rules and reality in dressage 75
Implications for fairness in judging 79
A welfare code incompatible with the reality of horse sport 81

7 **The impact of social media** 88
The emergence of 'rollkur' 89
YouTube and the impact of video 92

From 'rollkur' to 'hyperflexion' to 'LDR': plus ça change 100

8 Equestrian sport and media repression 103

'The riders don't feel comfortable with the camera' 104

FEI World Reining Finals: well that was awkward 105

'Take down that video!' 108

Intimidation of photographers at shows 110

Taking the fight to the courts 117

9 The price of more flags is declining safety 120

Logistical barriers limit opportunities to qualify 121

Standards in Equestrian's 'new markets' are still too low 123

Contrived universality may harm athlete safety and public opinion 125

10 The equestrian fanbase is overstated 129

As the sport bleeds fans, the side-show becomes more and more undignified 136

11 Equestrian will not meet modern standards. Will the IOC? 140

Fear of litigation limits officials' ability to enforce the rules 144

Conflicting views among member countries 146

Equestrian may not meet modern legal codes 149

Public exposure of abuse will only increase 150

Over to you, IOC 152

Bibliography 154

Preface

I AM WRITING THIS FOR 102 people I have never met. You are the members of the International Olympic Committee (IOC). It is you who possess the power, and therefore the responsibility, to end the participation of horses in the Olympic Games by discontinuing all equestrian disciplines as well as modern pentathlon.

Why would the IOC do such a thing? It really makes more sense to ask, why not? The increasing cost of hosting the Olympic Games is always an issue, and equestrian events are expensive to host and don't command a large audience. It is important to the future of the Games to include sports that appeal to a global, young audience, but despite efforts to make it more inclusive, Equestrian remains an elitist sport centred around wealthy people in Europe and North America. Income constraints and vital biosecurity measures prevent it from having any true potential for globality. Discontinuing Equestrian and modern pentathlon would free up eight events to include more relevant sports and disciplines at future Games.

The IOC is committed to ensuring the safety of athletes, and this is an important factor in maintaining public support. Equestrian is a dangerous sport, and some level of risk is accepted by all, but in recent years the efforts of the Fédération Équestre Internationale (FEI) to tailor its disciplines to conform to Olympic Agenda 2020 have seen riders and horses repeatedly endangered. A horse died in Tokyo from injuries sustained during competition, and others suffered predictable, preventable falls. Horses were seen bleeding and visibly distressed. Efforts to make Equestrian more accessible had led to some highly questionable qualification procedures, and young and inexperienced FEI riders were over-faced, humiliated and endangered on the altar of contrived universality. A modern pentathlon horse was flogged before the world. Seeing horses killed and riders over-faced is damaging to the public image and social license of the Olympic Games and is not something you should want to continue.

Clean sport and fair play are cornerstones of Olympism. As I will show, FEI horses necessarily run on drugs. So why aren't there more doping scandals? In a gross parody of WADA's Therapeutic Use Exemption rules, sick FEI horses can now compete on the same pain killers, sedatives and steroid hormones which cost Olympic medals and embarrassed the sport in the past. It would show true leadership and commitment to fair play for the IOC to vote to stop this charade from taking place in the name of the Olympic movement.

I have chosen to address the IOC in the form of an open letter, because the matter is very personal to me. It is personal to all of us who have been watching for decades while the values of the sport were abandoned, and its integrity eaten away. Former riders, coaches, veterinarians, officials, and most of all, former fans, now turn away in disgust and say or write the words: 'I can't watch anymore.' You can read these words again and again in the comment threads on social media. Written by members of a rapidly growing demographic: former equestrian insiders transformed, by their horror at seeing what is allowed by the sport's governing bodies, into informed and critical outsiders.

This letter is personal, but it is not just the private opinion of an individual lover of horses. I worked internationally as an equestrian journalist from 2005 to 2017. For most of those years, I worked closely with equine welfare and behaviour scientists to disseminate the latest evidence-based information about sustainable horse care. Much has changed for horses in recent years. Owners are more mindful of the needs of equines, and there is a growing trend internationally towards greater attention to the ethological needs of all domestic animals. Organisations that use animals to produce food or entertainment are increasingly obliged to improve animal welfare in order to maintain their social license, but at the elite, Olympic level, horse sport simply cannot conform to what are now understood to be the requirements of good horse care.

There was a time when I thought equestrian sport could get with the times and right its course. I thought the leaders of the FEI would make this happen, if only my colleagues and I showed them how badly the sport had strayed from its core values and how dire was the need to clean it up. Today, I know I was wrong. The FEI will never clean up equestrian sport because it is no longer possible to do so. All that is left for me to do is provide you with all the arguments you need to bring about its exit. Some of the documents I refer to have been removed from public access since I obtained them, but I have kept meticulous records, and all the evidence is available upon request.

All of the information in this book was already out in the world. What I have done is merely to compile, sort, and document what others and I have previously published. There is no way to ignore these facts or to wash one's hands of them. Not in the long term. In the words of Maya Angelou, when you know better, you do better. I wrote this book to be certain the members of the IOC know better. Then it will be up to you whether you do better.

1

Equestrian: a sport for all?

The promotion of equality, 'sport for all' and the spirit of fair play are part of the IOC mission, but the nature of Equestrian under the FEI falls far short of these ideals.

PART OF THE MISSION OF the IOC is 'to encourage and support the promotion and support of women in sport at all levels and in all structures with a view to implement the principle of equality of men and women'.[1] The FEI, too, markets itself to sponsors and the world in general as a leader in gender equality. One FEI promotion even claims 'total gender equality' in the sport.[2] This is because women have competed against men in Equestrian at the Olympic Games since 1952. It makes little sense to segregate events when the horses are the ones who supply the muscle power.

The myth of gender equality

However, slipping on a pair of riding boots does not—as advertised—cause patriarchal structures to melt away. If it were so, we should expect to see equestrian grassroots gender distribution reflected at the elite level.

1 IOC, Olympic Charter, 17 July 2020, 17.

2 FEI information sheet, 2019, https://inside.fei.org/system/files/Introducing_the FEI_continous_2019.pdf, accessed 18 Aug 2021.

That isn't the case. Whereas little boys are like hens' teeth at the average equestrian centre or livery yard, male representation increases with the level of competition. In sports governance, 72 percent of National Equestrian Federation presidents and secretaries general are male.[3] In Tokyo, the first Olympiad for which the IOC had achieved gender parity for athletes, I calculated that 35 percent of equestrians were female.

In dressage, the least popular of the three Olympic disciplines, women famously 'dominate'. In equestrian terms, this means that right before the Tokyo Olympics, 12 of the 20 highest-ranked dressage riders in the world were women.[4] In jumping, the most popular of the disciplines, 19 out of the 20 highest-ranking riders in the world at the same time were men.[5] In eventing, which is more popular than dressage but less popular than jumping, fourteen of the twenty highest-ranking riders globally were men.[6] In a sport where almost everyone at grassroots level is a woman or girl, that doesn't look much like 'total gender equality'.

Economic barriers to participation

Gender equality isn't the only kind of equality. The IOC also aims to encourage and support 'sport for all'; let us now examine how well the structures of the FEI accord with that goal. Equestrian has a reputation for being an elitist sport populated by minor royals and their Hooray Henry hangers-on, an image which is not entirely undeserved. It's a sticky wicket for the FEI. On the one hand, the sport must be seen to be inclusive if it wants to remain relevant at the Olympic Games. On the other hand, its

3 Gender equality statistics presented at FEI Sports Forum, 2019, 7, https://inside.fei.org/sites/default/files/SF19%20-%20Session%201%20Gender%20Equality%20SIB-15April2019_0.pdf, accessed 31 Aug 2021.

4 FEI, Official Dressage Rankings, 30 Jun 2021.

5 FEI, Longines Rankings, 30 Jun 2021.

6 FEI, Eventing World Athlete Rankings, 30 Jun 2021.

primary strength when selling to sponsors is its affluent fanbase. When national federations attend FEI briefings on how to market the sport to sponsors, they are advised to target luxury brands and to remind sponsors that equestrian fans tend to be rich and live in more affluent countries.

Dressage, jumping, and eventing are all capital-intensive events where success is inextricable, not just from the personal finances of each athlete, but also from the per-capita GDP of their country. Talented middle-class riders from affluent nations can do well at the Olympics aboard horses owned by syndicates or rich sponsors. In equestrian circles, this is often presented as proof that making it as an equestrian isn't all about money. The message seems to be that in addition to being rich—or knowing someone who is—successful athletes must also be better riders than all the other rich people. However, there is no getting around the fact that money is a major factor. In this way, hopeful equestrians are far from equal, and everyone in the sport knows this and tries not to talk about it too much, because everyone also knows that the IOC would like to see more diversity in Olympic sports. In the world of horse sport, stories of white middle-class riders winning medals at the Olympic Games are billed as rags to riches fairy tales, which underpin the narrative that Equestrian is for everyone. This Eurocentric fantasy rests on a highly exclusive definition of 'everyone.'

The comparative politics scholar Professor Danyel Reiche points out that 86.2 percent of Olympic Equestrian medals until and including 2016 had been taken by nations with a current per-capita GDP of above USD 20,000.[7] These statistics become even more striking if you disregard outlier Olympics like London 1948, when riders had not had the best opportunity to prepare their horses because of WWII, and requirements were therefore eased. In addition to the reduced difficulty

7 The following discussion of medal winning in relation to GDP is based on the figures in Danyel Reiche, *Success and Failure of Countries at the Olympic Games* (New York: Routledge, 2016), 69–70.

of the events, Germany was absent for obvious reasons. This led to unusual results. Many athletes also stayed away from Moscow 1980 in protest against the Soviet–Afghan war, again leaving others with increased chances of success.

The main beneficiary of the Moscow boycott from an equestrian perspective was the USSR, which won eight medals. Bulgaria and Romania also made rare appearances on the podium. Mexico won three of its total of seven equestrian medals in Moscow. The other four, it won in London in 1948. Without the results from 1948 and 1980, and including the medal statistics from Tokyo 2020, the share of dressage team medals won by nations with a current per-capita GDP of less than USD 20,000 is less than 6 percent. For eventing, it is 0 percent. For jumping, it is just over 6 percent. In the individual events, jumping looks the most inclusive, with five of 69 medals (about 7 percent) won by riders from poor nations. All but one of these medals were won before 1960. The most recent was taken by Brazil's Rodrigo Pessoa in Athens 2004. Pessoa, although representing Brazil, was born in Paris and grew up in Europe, where his father ran a successful training stable. He never lived in Brazil.

In individual dressage, athletes from poor nations have won four medals out of a total of 69: under 6 percent. Each of these medals was taken by an athlete representing the Soviet Union, and since 1980, only riders from rich nations have won dressage medals at the Olympic Games. Argentina's silver medal for individual eventing in 1964 brings the share of medals in this event for the less affluent countries to 1.5 percent. Out of a total of 380 medals won in over a century of Olympic Equestrian competitions since 1912 (excluding 1948 and 1980), only 15 (less than 4 percent) have been won by nations with a current per-capita GDP of under USD 20,000.

More flags does not really mean more participation in equestrian events

The FEI will likely point out that it is working very hard to include more flags at the Olympic Games, and that it now consists of no less than 136 affiliated national federations all over the world. This does not actually translate into more participation in equestrian events. The Ethiopian Equestrian Association, for example, has been affiliated with the FEI since 1997, but according to the FEI database as of July 2021, has never registered a single FEI athlete. Or a single horse. Even North Korea has an equestrian federation under the FEI. The DPR Korea Equestrian Association has no athletes, horses, officials nor even a website, and it shares its email address with other federations, such as the Weightlifting Association of the Democratic People's Republic of Korea and the Water Ski Association in Pyongyang. Over a third of affiliated national equestrian federations listed in the FEI's database had ten registered athletes or fewer in 2019.[8]

Then there is the curious case of the Equestrian Association of Iceland. Like the Ethiopian Equestrian Association, the Equestrian Association of Iceland has been affiliated with the FEI since 1997, but did not appear to have a single registered athlete or horse in 2019. This might sound strange, since Iceland is a country with a rich tradition of horsemanship and a per-capita GDP of over USD 73,000. However, it likely has something to do with the fact that importing horses into Iceland has been illegal for over a thousand years. Even horses born in Iceland can never return once they have been abroad. This means that the only horses present in Iceland are Icelandic ponies, who don't need to be registered with the FEI because their international competitions are organised by their own international federation, FEIF.

Why are these nations with little or no participation in FEI disciplines launching equestrian federations and affiliating? It's anyone's guess.

8 FEI, National Federations database, https://data.fei.org/NFPages/NF/Search, accessed Apr 2020.

According to the FEI's website, affiliating with the FEI entitles national federations to host international equestrian events according to the FEI rules, but why would Madagascar, for instance, want to host FEI shows? It has one athlete, and she lives in France, competes in France, previously represented France and, presumably, could represent France in the future. Angola hasn't hosted a single FEI event in its seven years of affiliation. Neither has Pakistan since it became affiliated in 1982. Over 20 percent of FEI affiliated national federations had never hosted an FEI competition as of 2020, according to the FEI's calendar of events.

With affiliation also comes the right to attend and vote at the annual FEI General Assembly. This begs the question: wherein lies the value of the opportunity to influence decisions about a sport which is little or not at all practised in your country?

One possible answer to that question is that affiliated federations can apply for funds and assistance for the development of equestrian sport in their nation. According to this somewhat inverted approach to 'supporting the grassroots', nations with little or no existing participation in FEI disciplines should form equestrian federations and affiliate with the FEI, so that the FEI can help them market equestrian sport to their citizens, so that they can (one day, maybe) register FEI riders and horses, so that they will eventually have a reason to care what decisions are made by the FEI General Assembly, thereby finding a use for their right to vote. In the meantime, international equestrian sport is governed by a federation with a one country, one vote democracy and a majority of voting officials at the General Assembly who have little or no experience with equestrian sport, let alone equestrian sports governance.

The FEI's curiously zealous global expansion efforts have long raised eyebrows within the ranks of its 'old' equestrian nations. In a discussion about the new format for equestrian team events at the Olympics, which took place during the International Jumping Riders Club General

Assembly in Rotterdam in August 2019, the President of the German Equestrian Federation, Count Breido zu Rantzau, made this comment:

> Ingmar [De Vos, FEI President] just said that the FEI and the national federations have decided. But I must say that in the General Assembly, there are about 140 nations, but a hundred don't really know anything about our sport. Only 20 or 30 people are trying to do the right thing. I think in this moment we have to say that. That cannot be the future of the FEI. Always with the non-riding countries making politics for the equestrian sport.[9]

The president of one of the world's biggest and oldest equestrian federations thinks that only about 20 percent of the national equestrian federations affiliated with the FEI have any business voting at the General Assembly, because the others are, as he puts it, 'non-riding countries'. Undermining the credibility of its own governance in order to impress the IOC is only one of many ways in which the FEI has enfeebled equestrian disciplines in its efforts to make it seem as if they are still suitable for the Olympic Games. In later chapters we will discuss how aside from playing the IOC for a bunch of fools, this strategy has completely ruined equestrian sport.

Later in 2019, during the FEI General Assembly in Moscow, as the members were about to vote on the affiliation of the national equestrian federations of the Bahamas, Mongolia and the Ivory Coast, it was the president of the Norwegian Equestrian Federation, Tore Sannum, who spoke out:

> I have no comments for the three new members, but in order to fall in line with other international federations, I think the FEI maybe could

9 International Jumping Riders Club, Video stream of panel debate during General Assembly, Facebook video, 22 Aug 2019, https://www.facebook.com/137022876422544/videos/1198035320378569, accessed 18 Aug 2021.

implement some new criteria for FEI membership. A national federation should prove its activity by competing at the level of the World Championships or the Olympic Games. And it must have a minimum number of athlete members, as happens in all other international federations. I also think it's important for the credibility of the sport and for our international federation in the eyes of the IOC, the press and the public. So I will ask the board to note this and maybe put that into criteria for next year.[10]

Promoting grassroots take-up of equestrian sport?

Once a newly minted national equestrian federation has affiliated with the FEI, it is eligible to apply for funds via FEI Solidarity. FEI Solidarity is the FEI's former Coaching Department, re-branded in 2011 as a charitable initiative to grow equestrian sport globally by 'providing the tools, the knowledge and the infrastructure required to develop the sport and nurture talent from grassroots to the world stage.' The programme rests on four pillars: 'the national federation', 'the athlete', 'the coach' and 'the values'. Put under the microscope, it does little to grow the sport among less privileged nations or individuals.

'The national federation' covers the training of sports administrators and officials as well as the development of IT solutions and infrastructure deemed necessary to run the sport nationally. Or unnecessary, as seems to be the case for The Horse Society of Botswana, which had no FEI events, no FEI horses and no FEI riders in 2019, but did have a national federation affiliated with the FEI, 10 officials, and an FEI Solidarity-funded website—which still had no content in 2021. 'The athlete' covers training and scholarships for riders. 'The coach' covers the certification and further education of coaches. And finally, 'the values' is an umbrella term for training support and service staff like farriers and grooms,

10 FEI General Assembly in Moscow, YouTube video, 19 Nov 2019, https://www.youtube.com/watch?v=XEXWqq1XbNI&t=2108s, accessed 18 Aug 2021.

providing riding lessons for poor or disabled persons, and donating money to existing projects which focus on horse health and welfare in rural communities.

According to FEI figures from 2019, 12 percent of FEI Solidarity funds so far have gone towards 'the values'.[11] That is the smallest entry. The largest is 'the coach' with 44 percent of FEI Solidarity funds going towards certifying and educating coaches. 'National federation' and 'athlete' have been allocated 25 percent and 19 percent of funds, respectively. The problem with this approach is that it does not (because it cannot) significantly address inequality within FEI disciplines. It does not matter how many coaches and officials and equestrian centres exist in a nation if that nation's people generally cannot afford to buy and keep performance horses. To benefit from FEI Solidarity, equestrian athletes must already be comparatively wealthy and connected within their society.

For instance, in Zambia, where almost 60 percent of the population live below the international poverty line of USD 1.90 per day, FEI Solidarity-subsidised coaching sessions begin at USD 35 per hour.[12] That's if you share a lesson with two other riders. Individual lessons with the FEI-provided national coach cost USD 90 per lesson. Before an athlete even gets as far as that, they must have a horse to ride, and they must be able to afford the services of farriers and saddlers. The result of this is that the photo galleries on the website of the Zambia National Equestrian Federation (ZANEF) give off a distinctly European and upper-middle-class vibe, despite the federation's six-year-long partnership with FEI Solidarity. This is a general trend for the FEI's activity in the African subcontinent, perhaps best exemplified by the official PR photograph of Team Africa

11 FEI, The FEI Solidarity Programme—FEI Course for NFs Secretaries General & Administrators, Lausanne (SUI) October 2019, https://zanef.com/app/uploads/2019/11/FEI-Services-Tools-FEI-Solidarity-Programme-2019.pdf.

12 ZANEF, Solidarity Coach recon document, 2017 ZANEF AGM, https://zanef.com/app/uploads/2017/01/ZANEF-AGM-2017-21-AGM-Solidarity-Coach-Recon-.pdf, accessed 19 Aug 2021.

published by the FEI in connection with the 2018 Youth Olympic Games.[13] From the team-members' names, looks, and backgrounds one would think the colonial era had never ended.

As part of ZANEF's deal with FEI Solidarity, it had also originally committed to providing riding lessons for underprivileged, indigenous Zambian children. However, this initiative is separate from the FEI Solidarity-funded sports development programme, and—as in the rest of the world—pales in comparison in terms of the money spent. Indeed, ZANEF seems to have struggled to spend more than roughly 10 percent of its earmarked budget each year the programme has been active. This has not stopped the FEI from declaring the Zambian Sports for All initiative a runaway watershed success.[14]

An FEI Solidarity press release from 2016 features apparently carefully posed indigenous Zambian children wearing riding apparel, and claims that the children are given 'new and exciting opportunities' by FEI Solidarity.[15] The Sports for All programme is breaking down barriers which only exist because of the false perception that Equestrian is an elitist sport, readers are told. That year, the ZANEF Chairperson's Report named the underprivileged children on whose behalf the federation's affiliated riding clubs had claimed financial support for lessons. On that list were just four names. In total, ZMW 14,850 (just under USD 1,500 at the exchange rate which applied at the fiscal year-end) had been spent on the Sports for All initiative in 2016, according to published ZANEF accounts.[16] That's only 13.5 percent of the ZMW 110,330 (approx. USD 11,000) planned for in the budget.

---

13 FEI, 'It's time for Africa', 29 Nov 2018, https://www.fei.org/stories/lifestyle/horse-human/africa-equestrian-solidarity, accessed 4 Sep 2021.

14 FEI, 'A mile in their shoes', press release, 9 Nov 2016, https://www.fei.org/stories/a-mile-in-their-shoes, accessed 18 Aug 2021.

15 FEI, 'A mile in their shoes'.

16 ZANEF Financial Report 2016, https://zanef.com/app/uploads/2017/01/AGM-2017-08-2016-Financial-Report.pdf, accessed 18 Aug 2021.

Meanwhile, the federation spent ZMW 127,805 (approx. USD 12,800) of FEI Solidarity money on flying in experts and putting on seminars, primarily for middle-class riders of European descent, whose dreams of going to the Olympic Games require assistance from the FEI. In 2017, ZANEF received a total of ZMW 124,491 (approx. USD 12,500) from FEI Solidarity, which was just under 60 percent of what the federation had expected according to its budget. That year, the Zambian Sports for All initiative so grippingly described in the FEI's press release the year before was set to invest ZMW 80,632 (approx. USD 8,000) in riding lessons for indigenous Zambian children. Less than 10 percent of that amount was actually used. Over ZMW 106,521 (approx. USD 10,500) of FEI Solidarity money was spent on training dressage officials and flying in the national coach for the jumping riders.[17]

In 2018, the budget for Sports for All in Zambia was ZMW 73,782 (approx. USD 6,000). Of that, ZMW 10,100 (approx. USD 850) was spent, according to the Treasurer's Report for the year.[18] All of it on sending a course builder to Germany to learn how to build jumps for riders who compete in FEI events. The absent expenditure for poor Zambian children was annotated in red: 'got to do something here'. The same year, the many thousands of dollars spent on coaching and educating riders from Zambia's minority of European descent finally paid off. A ZANEF FEI rider made it to the Youth Olympic Games. 'It's time for Africa' chanted equestrian social media users, echoing the FEI communications department. But it really isn't. At least not in the context of FEI Olympic disciplines.

There is no doubt that becoming an FEI Solidarity partner has transformed ZANEF. In 2019, the federation received ZMW 298,085 (approx. USD 21,000) in subsidies from the FEI. Its own income from

17 ZANEF Financial Report 2017, https://zanef.com/app/uploads/2018/02/AGM-2018-07-Financial-Report-2017-Budget-2018.pdf, accessed 19 Aug 2021.

18 ZANEF Financial Report 2018, https://zanef.com/app/uploads/2019/02/ZANEF-Accounts-2018-FOR-CIRCULARIZATIONxls-1.pdf, accessed 19 Aug 2021.

sources such as membership fees and horse registrations was only ZMW 200,835 (approx. USD 14,000). Before it became a beneficiary in 2015, the federation was treading water. Now—to borrow a phrase from former ZANEF chairperson Zara Nicolle—it has FEI Solidarity 'filling its coffers'. In a sport where money is everything, that translates into results for those who can afford to profit from the assistance. But the level playing field—if we are to include all human beings in that definition—is still not on the immediate horizon.

This is not to imply that there is anything wrong with an international athletic federation boosting its disciplines in regions remote from its epicentre. There is also nothing wrong with introducing poor children to horses. But the continuity between those two activities is contrived by the FEI to make it seem as if all that is necessary for equestrian sport to become mainstream in low- and middle-income countries is the right infrastructure and some more officials. That is not true. Unless the FEI has a plan to solve world poverty it does not have a plan to make its disciplines equally accessible to everyone, not even at the most basic grassroots level, and certainly not in the context of the Olympic Games.

Poverty-washing PR is demeaning and potentially harmful

The FEI's efforts to shed its elitist reputation have resulted in some press releases which would have embarrassed White Saviour Barbie herself. The Zambian story is only one example. In the Caribbean, the FEI claims to be 'Bringing Hope to Haiti' with a story published on its website in February 2018 about a young Haitian rider who made it to the Youth Olympic Games.[19] That does admittedly sound amazing. Haiti is the poorest country in the Western Hemisphere, and—as in Zambia—close

19 FEI, 'How Equestrianism is Bringing Hope to Haiti', 27 Feb 2018, https://www.fei.org/stories/lifestyle/horse-human/equestrianism-haiti-hope, accessed 19 Aug 2021.

to 60 percent of its people live below the international poverty line. However did this incredible young athlete achieve such an impressive result against such odds? Firstly, he was born into one of Haiti's wealthiest and most influential families. Secondly, he doesn't live in Haiti: he lives in Florida. And thirdly, this promising athlete rides performance-bred sport horses imported from Europe, which are completely out of reach to the average Haitian. To claim this young man's case as evidence of FEI sport taking off in Haiti is a stretch.

The press release about Haiti is accompanied by a stirring FEI Solidarity video from 2015. It is tempting to write something snarky to mock this film, but it is impossible to think of anything as effective as simply quoting the introductory voice-over:

> Haiti is an island nation with a unique history of resilience. The Haitian people staged the only true successful slave rebellion. They have learned to overcome much. Most recently, they endured the island rending earthquake of 2010, that paralysed the nation and flattened much of the beautiful city of Port-au-Prince. Once again, the Haitians have prevailed.[20]

You are probably on the edge of your seat, waiting to discover what transformational event has occurred in Haiti to warrant comparison to the country's revolution in 1804 and the earthquake in 2010. I have watched the entire video segment, so you don't have to. The event referred to is an FEI Solidarity sponsored course for grooms, aimed at improving their ability to look after their employers' horses. The FEI includes training courses for support staff in its solidarity programme, because it knows that, as far as poor people are concerned, stuffing hay nets and scooping up horse manure is the maximal feasible level of participation in international

20 FEI, 'Equestrian Snapshots—Haitian Equestrian Federation' YouTube video, 24 Mar 2015, https://www.youtube.com/watch?v=F8ymfl661OU&feature=emb_title, accessed 19 Aug 2021.

equestrian sport. If that reads like hyperbole to you, pay attention to the words of the FEI Solidarity instructor flown to Haiti to teach the course. This quote is also from the video:

> I think today our sport, the sport of showjumping, eventing, dressage, driving, reining and endurance has become global and that is the key word, global. So we have to help the development of the grassroots and the development programmes in order for them to reach the top. And with this grooms' course, I can see very, very soon some of the guys I have here could definitely be going to Florida to groom for some of the top riders and that's what we need.

The statement poses more questions than it answers. How easy is it to work as a top international groom, jetting back and forth between Miami and Amsterdam and zipping over national borders every week while you're in Europe, when you hold one of the most restricted passports in the world? Don't they already have grooms in Florida? And if the reason for training grooms in Haiti is really that equestrian sport 'has become global', why aren't the grooms needed in their home country? The last one is a rhetorical question—the Florida based Youth Olympian was, at the time the press release and video were published, the only Haitian rider competing in FEI events. Since the Federation Équestre Haitienne affiliated with the FEI in 1999, there have been only four others.

Horses aren't just expensive to acquire. Their upkeep—if they are expected to perform in competitions—is what really breaks the bank. Feed costs money, and if you don't want to risk falling foul of the anti-doping rules, you have to use one of the premium brands which are screened for contaminants. If you were an average Haitian person with a single FEI horse, you could spend your entire annual income just on bags of horse feed in less than four months. Should you be unlucky and find yourself embroiled in a doping case because of contamination, the legal fees to clear your name could be thousands of dollars. Quality hay isn't readily available everywhere in the world, and it is also very expensive when it has to be shipped. Haiti struggles with water shortages and frequent droughts. A sport horse in full training in a hot climate can drink 75 litres of water per day. The list of things Haitians need is undoubtedly long. It is questionable whether equestrian industry growth is on that list.

Stabling costs a lot of money. Horses need their hooves maintained by a trained farrier at least every six weeks. Saddles for horse sport cost thousands of dollars and have to be fitted and regularly re-fitted to each horse by a master saddler. Domestic horses must see the dentist at least once per year, because their lifestyle causes problems with their teeth. Competition horses develop musculoskeletal problems and must be regularly monitored and treated by specialist veterinarians, as well as physiotherapists, masseurs and other body workers. Diagnostic imaging techniques routinely used for the investigation of pathology in performance horses include MRI, scintigraphy, ultrasonography and radiography. Horses even have CT scans now. The demands of elite equestrian sport lead to horses needing regular medical treatment of a standard that is not even available to most humans on the planet.

In Haiti, as in other places, FEI Solidarity latches onto existing, local projects—like riding for the disabled and health support for working horses—and squeezes every ounce of public relations value out of its donations. But none of that changes the basic truth about Olympic participation in equestrian sport: It is inherently inaccessible to people who are poor. Just consider the cost of transporting horses. Depending on the discipline, top riders compete on several continents. From Wellington, to St Tropez, to Doha; the locations vary, but the names of the riders are the same. Horses travel by air, accompanied by grooms, and of course, you cannot have just one horse if you want to be taken seriously as a professional. You need several. Even in Denmark, where the standard of living is among the highest in the world, and municipal riding schools in every town make riding lessons accessible to most people, FEI sport is still mainly for those who have money or connections or both. In one international championship, the Danish dressage team included a member of the royal family, the son of the President of the Danish Equestrian Federation, and the daughter of the main sponsor of the championships. I have not worked out the odds of that happening in Athletics, but I suspect they are quite low.

Unless you can afford to be a rider, your participation in international horse sport is likely to consist of mucking out stables and tacking up horses for those who can.

Abuse of power in equestrian sport

Unequal access to horses is unfair in a sporting sense, but it can also be wielded as a weapon of oppression. Since the U.S. Center for Safe Sport started investigating cases of sexual misconduct in 2017, one scandal after another has rattled the equestrian scene in the United States. The *New York Times* has run exposés on two of the most legendary figures in U.S. showjumping history, Jimmy Williams and George Morris.[21] Both have been accused of sexually inappropriate behaviour involving minors, and in 2019, Safe Sport added Olympic jumping medallist and former chef d'équipe of the United States jumping team, George Morris, to the list of 'permanently ineligible' coaches. Famed trainer of multiple Olympic riders, Jimmy Williams, who has been accused of raping girls as young as 11, died in 1993.

21 Sarah Maslin Nir, 'Whispers of Sexual Abuse Tailed an Equestrian Legend for Decades. At 81, He Was Barred for Life', New York Times, 8 Aug 2019, https://www.nytimes.com/2019/08/08/sports/george-morris.html, accessed 19 Aug 2021; and 'The Equestrian Coach Who Minted Olympians, and Left a Trail of Child Molestation', *New York Times*, 29 May 2019, https://www.nytimes.com/2018/05/29/sports/jimmy-williams-flintridge.html?module=inline,accessed 19 Aug 2021.

Both men were considered kings among Olympic coaches. Just as in other disciplines, the coach who is known to create Olympic athletes in dressage, jumping or eventing holds unimaginable power over young hopefuls. This is even more intensely true for equestrian disciplines than for any other, because the most talented rider stands little chance of making it without that special horse. Finding favour with a fashionable coach is a way for the children of ordinary people to gain access to expensive horses owned by syndicates and sponsors. One of George Morris' accusers, Jonathan Soresi, was not from a wealthy family, but dreamt of equestrian greatness. 'There was an underlying hope,' he said to the *New York Times*, 'that if I went along with this, I would get what I did not have, which was horses and education.'[22]

In December 2017, the equestrian news website Eventing Nation published an anonymous letter by a survivor of sexual abuse. The letter is written for her younger self and details how she endured inappropriate sexual behaviour from her coach out of fear of losing that good horse she had been given to ride and who was supposed to 'take her to the next level':

> Molestation is an ugly word, so you don't use it—after all, it isn't like you are kicking and screaming to get away. Another word you don't use is 'no,' and as a result you feel responsible for the blurring of boundaries. You feel complicit. Besides which, what if you tell someone and the nice horse gets taken away, or your parents take away horses altogether? None of these seem like risks worth taking, so it goes on, for years.[23]

Five-times Olympian Anne Kursinski is currently the most high-profile sexual abuse survivor in equestrian sport. Ms Kursinski blew the whistle

22 Nir, 'Whispers of Sexual Abuse'.

23 Eventing Nation, '#MeToo: A Letter to Myself as a Young Rider', 15 Dec 2017, https://eventingnation.com/metoo-a-letter-to-myself-as-a-young-rider/, accessed 19 Aug 2021.

on Jimmy Williams in an interview with *Chronicle of the Horse*, and later spoke out to the *New York Times*. The newspaper interviewed 38 sources who had been at the Flintridge Riding Club where Williams was the star trainer: riders, grooms, officials and other members. According to the article, they described 'a toxic brew of prestige and ambition that led parents, bent on their child's success in the show ring, to ignore his near daily predations—and persuaded children who were afraid of losing beloved horses to stay silent.'[24]

This fear of 'losing beloved horses' illustrates why the disproportionate power held by equestrian coaches (and wealthy horse owners) who control athletes' access to horses is not limited to the upper levels of horse sport. Every local riding school is full of children and youngsters who would do almost anything not to be cut off from that 'beloved horse', whether it refers to a top dressage mount or a woolly pony. While working as an equestrian journalist, I spoke to many young grooms and pupils who had stories to tell. Not necessarily of sexual assault, but of topics like horse abuse, cheating, doping, and fraud. Often, what prevented them from speaking on the record was fear that they could no longer see a horse whom they felt depended on them. In one case, an ex-groom who called me was worried that the coach she was accusing of insurance fraud would punish her by deliberately hurting her favourite horse.

In this way, inequality is woven into the fabric of equestrian sport from top to bottom, because it is impossible to make it on talent and hard work alone. There are always some people who control access to the horses whom other people want to ride, be around or even help and protect. The FEI knows this but does not seem to mind. One of the theoretical models of a 'typical fan', with which the FEI's commercial department operates, is a 10-year-old girl called 'Mary'. Mary is from a low-income family, and she can't afford a horse, so every day she works for someone

24 Nir, 'The Equestrian Coach Who Minted Olympians'.

who can, in return for their permission to ride. While in other sports, adults give their own free time to help children at grassroots level, in equestrian sport, making young children perform menial labour for the chance to participate in recreational sport is considered so normal it has made it into the marketing manuals of the FEI. At every level, access is about money. But nowhere is that more true than it is for those with Olympic ambitions. While 'Mary' cleans boots and sweeps the yard for the occasional chance of a ride, another young girl is bought a Grand Prix horse by her parents and carried off to the Olympic Games.

Is it in accord with the Olympic ideal of solidarity to include events which can essentially only be won by the world's richest and their cherrypicked favourites? Is it fair play that someone with little or no international experience can qualify for the Olympic Games the same year they begin to compete on a horse worth millions of euros? A horse who has been trained for them by somebody else? That is for you to decide, but if there exists a valid defence of Equestrian as worthy of continued Olympic status, it is definitely not that the sport promotes equality.

2

Animals in the Olympics are a liability, not an asset

In recent decades, Equestrian events have been marketed as showing a close and admirable bond between horse and rider, with horses described as 'partners' and 'athletes'. Yet the pressure of modern competition is such that the horse is treated far more as a piece of sporting equipment than as a partner.

EQUESTRIAN IS THE ONLY OLYMPIC sport in which non-human animals participate. The Fédération Équestre Internationale refers to the horse-human dyad as a 'unique sporting partnership built on mutual trust and respect.' This definition is included in the federation's core values and is strongly emphasised in the FEI's promotion of the sport. In reality, sport horses are heavily commodified and have no agency over their participation in Olympic disciplines. In a world rapidly turning its back on the use of non-human animals for human entertainment, what was once considered a strong selling point has now turned into an unsolvable predicament, not unlike elephants in the circus.

Before the Olympic Games in London 2012, organisers faced criticism from six leading animal rights groups when it was announced that the opening ceremony would feature live farm animals as part of a pastoral

Great Britain theme. Under the 2006 Animal Welfare Act, it is forbidden to intentionally cause undue fear and distress to animals, and it was thought by the animal rights groups, including Viva! and Freedom for Animals, that the opening ceremony as proposed would be illegal under the Act.[1]

Plans to display captive orca in Sochi during the 2014 Winter Olympic Games were abandoned after protests from animal advocates, and in 2016, organisers for the Rio Games were forced to apologise after a female jaguar named Juma was shot in connection with her appearance in an Olympic torch relay. 'We made a mistake in permitting the Olympic torch, a symbol of peace and unity, to be exhibited alongside a chained wild animal. This image goes against our beliefs and our values,' said the organisers.[2]

Given the press faced by previous Olympic Games over animal exploitation, and the row over the lack of animal welfare standards in catering for the Olympics in Tokyo (overshadowed by COVID-19 concerns, but by no means forgotten), trying to frame the FEI's use of live animals in sport as a positive selling point appears to be too optimistic. Athletes now openly speak against the use of factory-farmed animal ingredients in food served at the Olympics. In an open letter to the Organising Committee of the Tokyo Olympic Games, a list of Olympians, headed up by US Olympic silver-medal-winning cyclist Dotsie Bausch, requested that the food served to athletes during the games be 'sourced from free roaming animals'.[3] Bausch and her co-signatories cited the

1 Owen Gibson, 'Danny Boyle urged to drop live animals from Olympics opening ceremony', *The Guardian*, 22 Jun 2012, https://www.theguardian.com/sport/2012/jun/22/danny-boyle-animals-olympics, accessed 19 Aug 2021.

2 Reuters, 'Amazon jaguar shot dead after Olympic torch ceremony', 21 Jun 2016, https://www.reuters.com/article/olympics-rio-jaguar-idUKL8N19D5AY, accessed 19 Aug 2021.

3 Legacy for Animals, 'What We Request' (open letter to the Governor of Tokyo and the Tokyo Organising Committee of the Olympic and Paralympic Games), Aug 2018, https://legacyforanimals.com/en/tag/dotsie-bausch/, accessed 19 Aug 2021.

precedent set by the London and Rio games, both of which had minimum standards regarding production animal welfare. If athletes are increasingly uncomfortable participating in events that serve battery eggs—or bacon from gestation crates—it is reasonable to assume that some will object when they learn that the life of an Olympic-level sport horse is far from cage free.

Animal exploitation and the Olympic brand

A major talking point during the Tokyo Olympics was the ordeal suffered by a modern pentathlon horse named Saint Boy. His German rider was seen whipping him, kicking him with her spurs, and hurting his mouth by yanking on the reins. The video initially gained attention because Saint Boy's refusal to obey cost the athlete her gold medal. But soon, horse lovers and non-horse people alike were agreeing on social media platforms that what they had just witnessed at the Olympic Games was nothing short of animal abuse. The German Animal Welfare Federation, which is the umbrella organisation for animal welfare associations and animal shelters in Germany, and has over 800,000 members, has since filed criminal charges against the athlete and her coach.[4] According to the federation's president, Thomas Schröder, 'animals have no place in a performance orientated competition between people.'

People for the Ethical Treatment of Animals (PETA) wrote an open letter to IOC President Thomas Bach, demanding that all events involving horses be banned from the Olympic Games. In France and Germany, animal welfare-focused political parties called for an end to all

4 Deutscher Tierschutzbund, 'Deutscher Tierschutzbund erstattet Anzeige gegen Fünfkämpferin Annika Schleu und ihre Trainerin' [The German Animal Welfare Federation files criminal charges against pentathlete Annika Schleu and her trainer], 13 August 2021, https://www.tierschutzbund.de/news-storage/heimtiere/130821-pferdemisshandlung-bei-olympia-deutscher-tierschutzbund-stellt-strafanzeige-gegen-trainerin-und-reiterin, accessed 4 Sep 2021.

use of horses in sport. The Italian Horse Protection Society did the same.

The FEI events were also criticised on social media and by the riders themselves for putting too much pressure on the horses. There was no shortage of terrible publicity for the Tokyo Olympic Games where Equestrian was concerned. A dressage horse was eliminated for bleeding from the mouth. A jumping horse was bloodied by the rider's spur. Preventable and predictable horse falls happened in both eventing and jumping because of the new team format.

The fact that horses are used in equestrian sport is not a feature. It's a bug and the FEI knows that it may be the bug that ends the sport, because the federation has been told so repeatedly over the years by its own experts. Chief Executive Roly Owers, from the FEI's partner organisation World Horse Welfare, has spoken at several FEI meetings about social licence to operate, the 'unwritten, non-legally binding contract' by which 'society "gives" right to operate', as Dr Owers puts it in his advice to the FEI. At the Willinga Park Equestrian Conference Centre in New South Wales, Australia, Dr Owers told delegates at a 2020 FEI Regional Dressage Forum:

> You and I are both of that view that we have a partnership with our horses. But there are those animal activists who believe increasingly that it's exploitation, especially of animals in horse sport. There is a growing view that, rather than 'use, not abuse', there's a growing view that all use of equines is abuse.

Dr Owers went on to warn delegates that horse sport might become illegal, unless the social licence to operate were made a priority. He cited the case of greyhound racing, which was banned in New South Wales for a period because animal welfare concerns caused the public to withdraw its social licence to operate. Dr Owers mentioned that protesters had disrupted the European Jumping Championships in Rotterdam in 2019, and that he foresaw many more such stories making it into the media. According to Dr Owers, there was little or no hope that equestrian sport would ever have the highest degree of social licence to operate. But there was a way to improve the sport's image to a level where it would be allowed to continue:

> People's association with equine welfare is mostly negative because those are the stories that they hear about. And that's why it's so important that we are far better at articulating the ethical basis for using horses for sport. It's a relationship and that means it's two way and therefore there's a balance to that. [5]

No evidence horses want to compete

So the ethical basis for using horses for sport, according to Dr Owers, is that this use is based on a mutual and balanced relationship between horse and human. Or, as FEI president Ingmar De Vos expresses it: 'Equestrian sport is all about the connection, intuitive link and committed partnership between the two athletes, which make our sport one of the most compelling at the Olympic Games.'[6]

The problem with this narrative is that there is quite a lot of evidence that it is false and no evidence that it is true. Even Dr Owers admitted in his talk at the FEI meeting at Willinga Park that equestrians can provide no solid evidence to support their claims that horses 'love' being used in competitions. Meanwhile, peer-reviewed published scientific studies are

5 Dr Roly Owers, 'A social license for equestrian sport', YouTube video of talk at FEI regional meeting, 29 Apr 2020, https://www.youtube.com/watch?v=OtWcN1N13TQ&t=12s, timecode 48:00, accessed 19 Aug 2021.

6 FEI, 'Olympic equestrian #TwoHearts campaign captures hearts around the world', press release, 17 May 2016, https://inside.fei.org/media-updates/olympic-equestrian-twohearts-campaign-captures-hearts-around-world, accessed 19 Aug 2021.

piling up which indicate that horses are very much not enjoying their role in equestrian sport, or the lifestyle that comes with it.

If using horses for sport were really about 'the connection' and some 'intuitive link', we should not expect to see the world's elite riders using coercive tools and methods to make horses do their bidding. In what other Olympic sport is it considered acceptable for an athlete to communicate with their team-mate by kicking them with a metal stud or hitting them with a stick? In what other Olympic sport are points given for 'submission' and penalties for 'disobedience' within the team?

If equestrians relied on a 'committed partnership' with their horses in order to succeed, we should not expect to see FEI horses touted like tickets to sporting fame. However, a good horse can do wonders for a rider's chances of becoming an Olympian, and good horses are available to anyone who can afford them. Upscale horse traders joke about how they're looking for a particularly good horse because 'this one has to go to the Olympic Games with [name of notoriously unskilled wealthy person]'.

If the road to equestrian greatness really relied on committed partnerships, we should not expect to see riders on the podium at the Olympic Games accepting medals for riding horses trained by someone else and acquired only at the last minute. At London 2012, one medallist had ridden his very first FEI competition on his horse less than one month before the Olympics. The horse had been acquired seven months earlier from the rider who had brought him on to Olympic level.

How insulting it must be to athletes who have worked their entire lives just to compete in the Olympic Games that in Rio, as well as in London, Hong Kong, and Tokyo, medals were won in Equestrian by people who lacked the patience or skill or both to qualify on a horse whom they had trained themselves. This is a common, industry-wide practice and it is openly reported in the equestrian press when a rider or their sponsor acquires a ready-made Grand Prix horse in order to be able to qualify for the Olympics. This is just how it is in equestrian sport. You don't have to agree or disagree with it. But you do have to decide whether it makes for a convincing backdrop to the narrative that FEI sport is about committed partnerships between riders and their horses.

I once saw a rider at an FEI show win a prize from the sponsor of the competition. The prize was a piece of equipment designed to give horses an electric shock when they kick at the walls of the stable in frustration at not being able to leave. If horses were really partners, their riders and the FEI would consider such a sponsorship unacceptable, let alone such a prize. If horses were considered partners, eating them after they cease to be competitive would not be on the World Horse Welfare list of acceptable retirement plans.

If horses were regarded as athletes, I could go to Olympics.com and search for Salinero or Authentic or Charisma under 'Athletes' and find that they had dedicated pages. They do not. I suspect it is because you, who sit on the IOC, already don't believe that horses are really athletes. They are only considered athletes on a par with riders when this construct serves a public relations purpose for the FEI: namely that of making it appear as if horses compete at the Olympic Games for reasons of their own, which—of course—they don't.

Equestrians invent personae for their horses, akin to the ones children make up for their stuffed animals, but these characters are fantasies. The horse's real personality is rarely allowed to be expressed, because such expression is usually inconvenient for the rider. Instead, human ambitions and prejudices are projected onto the horses. Their animal natures are repressed, and they are re-invented as anthropomorphised 'athletes' who understand the purpose of equestrian sport, want to win and, conveniently, don't seem to care about the sorts of things other horses evolved to need, such as moving around freely or belonging to a bonded social group. It is important to keep in mind that when a rider talks about their horse as someone who 'loves to compete', that is nothing but a projection of their own social conditioning and wishful thinking.

In his classic, *Kinship with all Life*, J. Allen Boone writes about Mojave Dan, a man who lives in harmony with Nature and his nomadic family of dogs and burros. When the author is frustrated in his attempts to bond with Strongheart, a famous canine movie star entrusted to his care, he seeks advice from Mojave Dan. 'There's facts about dogs, and there's opinions about them,' replies Dan. 'The dogs have all the facts, and the humans have all the opinions.'[7] This is also true of horses. If you want to know something about a horse, it's no use asking their rider. You have to ask the horse, and you have to be willing to accept their answer.

Horses express themselves primarily through body language. Most equestrian equipment is designed to prevent them from doing so. There are tools to force the horse's head down when the horse wants to carry it high. There are tools to force the head up when the horse wants to put it down low. There are tools to prevent frightened horses from running away, and there are tools to force tired horses to move. There are tools to keep horses from bucking or rearing to defend themselves against their riders. There are tools to strap their mouths shut so they can't escape the pressure from the bits. And when chronically stressed horses develop repetitive behaviours as coping mechanisms, there are tools to mask their symptoms, either by punishment or by mechanical restraint. Understanding what horses are expressing is not just about understanding their body language. It is at least as much about having the courage to really listen to what they are saying. Even if you don't like what you hear.

One powerful indicator of the true status of horses within horse sport is that the animal rights movement is regarded by equestrians with terror and hostility. This gives rise to the question: why would someone not want their committed athletic partner, with whom they share an intuitive relationship, to have legal rights? Wouldn't they push to ensure their best

7 J. Allen Boone, *Kinship With All Life*, (San Francisco, Harper, 1954), 47.

friend obtained personhood? In what other Olympic sport would athletes want to freeze a team-mate in the role of legal object?

The obvious and often dreaded destination of animal rights thinking is that an empowered horse will be entitled to refuse to participate in equestrian sport or even leisure riding. Deep down, most equestrians suspect that their horses would exercise such a right if given the chance. In the words of Dr Owers, when he spoke at an FEI conference on doping rules in 2010: 'Let us always remember that the horse does not have a choice whether or not to compete in horse sport.' This knowledge—that horses didn't vote for horse sport—and the belief that 'horses love to compete', coexist uneasily in the minds of equestrians.

For the purposes of this argument, you needn't agree or disagree with the animal rights movement. The question here is not whether animal exploitation is good or bad. The question is, whether the description of the horse-human relationship in equestrian sport as a mutual partnership is accurate.

In his social licence talk, Dr Owers differentiates between using horses and exploiting them. But what is the difference, if there is any, between use and exploitation? According to the Cambridge Dictionary, 'exploit' as a verb can have two different meanings: 'to use something in a way that helps you'; and 'to use someone or something unfairly for your own advantage.' Use and exploit are synonyms. Both words can be neutral when applied to an object. 'I am using this hammer.' 'I am exploiting this opportunity.' When applied to a subject, to someone, they each take on negative connotations. 'You used your ex-boyfriend.' 'You exploited your employees.'

Equestrian sport faces many paradoxes, and this is one: if horses are regarded morally as persons, then using them takes on a whiff of exploitation. If horses are regarded morally as objects, then the idea of a horse-human 'partnership' is nonsense.

If horses wanted to win ribbons, we should never expect to see them refuse a jump or try to run around it. We should not expect to see horses kick at the rider's legs or try to wrestle free of the reins. If horses wanted to compete, we should not expect them to swish their tails, resist the rider or attempt to open their mouths in dressage. Judges are, at least in theory, supposed to mark down these behaviours. Yet, they occur roughly every five seconds at elite FEI level, according to one study.[8]

When a horse's bridle accidentally comes off during the routine tack check after a dressage test, as it happened in Aachen in 2017, we should not expect that horse to take the opportunity to make his escape. A horse who considered himself the partner of his rider, among friends, and in the middle of an important competition would just stand there and wait for the bridle to be sorted out. Like a runner who had dropped a shoe.

If horses understood or cared about international championships, we should not expect them to be frightened by the medal-giving ceremony. A champion horse who understood the significance of the situation would line up proudly next to their rider and accept the adoration of the crowds. Horses would not have to be led around in little circles, fidgeting and pulling faces because they couldn't stand still. They would never rear up and strike their grooms in the face like one medal-winning German horse did in Rio 2016.

'Ah, but horses are unpredictable.' That's what equestrians will tell you. Horses are no less predictable than humans. If you put a human in a situation that is frightening and difficult for them, and which they would rather not be in, they will—predictably—try to leave. Horses are the same.

---

8 Aleksandra Gorecka-Bruzda, 'Conflict behaviour in elite show jumping and dressage horses', *Journal of Veterinary Behaviour Clinical Applications and Research*, 10/2 (2014), https://www.researchgate.net/publication/271226102_Conflict_behavior_in_elite_show_jumping_and_dressage_horses, accessed 19 Aug 2021. doi:10.1016/j.jveb.2014.10.004.

Special reins are allowed at prize giving ceremonies for jumping, which operate through a pulley system and which are not otherwise allowed in the competition arena, because they are considered too severe. Such reins are used at medal ceremonies for safety reasons, to prevent horses from escaping the control of their riders or handlers. Dressage riders are allowed to carry a whip to the prize giving. Just in case. If horses understood or cared why they were there, none of this would be necessary.

In what other Olympic sport must athletes employ mechanical restraints to prevent their team-mates from fleeing the medal ceremony? In that sense, equestrian sport really is as unique as the FEI claims. It is also unique in that it is the only Olympic sport where an athlete can be the legal owner of their team-mate. It is unique in that a former Olympic 'athlete' who has won team gold and individual silver can be sold at a bankruptcy auction with no reserve.[9] It is unique in that it is the only Olympic sport where an athlete may 'correct' their team-mate's behaviour with a whip or a sharp poke in the ribs with a metal stud. It is unique in that it is the only Olympic sport where an athlete may sell their team-mate to the highest bidder or retire them to the glue factory. It is unique. It just isn't unique in any way that justifies its continued status as an Olympic sport. As the following chapters will demonstrate, the 'unique sporting partnership built on mutual trust and respect' proclaimed by the FEI to be one of its core values is dispiritingly absent in the world of elite equestrian sport.

9 Carol Phillips, 'Carl Hester "appalled" by sale of Uthopia by auction', *Horse & Hound*, 28 April 2016, https://www.horseandhound.co.uk/news/carl-hester-appalled-sale-uthopia-auction-533937, accessed 4 Sep 2021.

3

Modern horse sport does not represent tradition

'It's an Olympic tradition' is not a good enough reason to keep including an event, when the regulators of the sport have long since stopped paying more than lip-service to its traditions.

SOMETIMES WE HUMANS—AS INDIVIDUALS AND as peoples—cling for far too long to impractical or even gruesome habits, because we are in love with the idea of tradition. In the case of equestrian sport, however, there is no dilemma to negotiate. The traditions, values, and founding philosophy of the sport have already been stripped out and sold for parts by the FEI over the decades. There is nothing of cultural or historical interest left to guard.

It is true that people have been riding horses for thousands of years. It is true that the ancient Olympics included equestrian events. And it is true that horse sport has been part of the modern Olympics for over a century. Whether these facts justify the inclusion of Equestrian at future Olympics depends on the answers to the following three questions: does tradition automatically justify the existence of any Olympic sport? If yes, does modern horse sport really preserve the traditions of classical horsemanship? If it does, are these traditions worthy of preservation?

Unless the answer to all three questions is yes, the appeal to tradition so often made by the sport's defenders is invalid.

The first question is the easiest one to answer. Should Equestrian automatically be included in future Olympics, simply because it was included in the past? The answer to that is surely a no. Sports and disciplines have been discontinued before. Even sports and disciplines that used horses. Polo was contested at five Olympics between 1900 and 1936. Paris 1900 had the high jump. Vaulting made an appearance in 1920 and then disappeared. There is no precedent for holding on to events, simply because they are old, whether or not there are horses in the picture.

Traditional horsemanship and modern competition

This leads to the second question. Does modern horse sport really preserve the traditions of classical horsemanship as it claims to do? To answer this question, one must first know a little bit of equestrian history. The cavalries of pre-mechanised Europe demanded a steady stream of horses fit to be sent to war, with soldiers on their backs who were not necessarily expert riders. Systems were in place to transform young horses into steady, durable mounts who were easy to ride, could travel far without becoming lame, and who could keep their calm when faced with the terrors of war.

In peacetime, battle drums would be played in the stable at feeding time to help horses habituate to their sound. A young horse who was just beginning training would be given a piece of bread after each day's schooling session, and the treat would be preceded by a loud crack of the whip. Later, a pistol shot would sound before the morsel was given to the horse, and eventually the pistol would be fired from the saddle before the horse received their bread. The treat would be given to the horse with the same hand that had fired the pistol, so that the experience would include both the sound and smell of gunfire. All of this served the purpose of building up the horse's resilience to the sensory experiences of battle. It was done systematically through Pavlovian conditioning long before Ivan Pavlov ever rang his bell.

Protocols also existed for the physical education of the young horses, or remounts as they were called. Documents from around the turn of the 20th century describe these processes, whereby the young horses, initially finding it difficult to balance with a human on their backs, were exercised over natural terrain, as well as over little jumps, for several months, while their strength and balance adapted to their new burden. The horse's natural inclination to follow other horses was used in this work. As long as an experienced horse went ahead, the riders on the young horses would not need to do much steering, but could focus on making themselves as unobtrusive passengers as possible.

The necessity for this gradual gymnastic work was that a horse naturally carries most of their weight on the front legs. When a rider mounts, this adds further to the load on the front legs and the strange sensation of having someone sitting on their back also makes a young horse tense. This tension and loss of balance disrupts the fluidity and rhythm of the horse's movement, which—in time—adds unnecessary wear and tear to their body.

The early schooling of cavalry horses allowed them to re-discover their natural relaxation and balance under a rider on straight lines. The pure rhythm of the gaits was considered the basis for all riding because any disruption of that rhythm was interpreted as a sign of tension. As their abilities developed, and as a horse's back and hind legs grew stronger and more able to carry weight, curved lines could be incorporated, whereby the inside hind leg had to take more weight than that on the outside. Whereas, in the early days, the job of the rider was to follow the horse's movements, stronger horses grew increasingly able to follow any shifts in balance initiated by the rider.

By riding on circles and eventually through what is known as lateral movements, the horse's hind legs and loins could be further strengthened and suppled, eventually rendering some horses able to jump large obstacles or perform the most demanding dressage movements under rider. This level of advancement took years to reach. It was not necessary for the average cavalry horse, but the ability to perform at advanced level was built on the foundation of the basic education of military horses, also known as campaign riding.

In its infancy, equestrian sport was only open to cavalry officers, and a spirit of fierce purism distinguished it from 'the circus.' Circus riding was considered to be the type of riding which was performed for money in front of an uninitiated audience. Circus riders could not rely on their non-military audience to understand the subtle finesse of dressage schooling, and so their performances were, by necessity, spectacular displays without any gymnastic value for the horse. General Decarpentry, co-author of the original FEI Dressage Rules, wrote of the difference between what he saw as equestrian art and the 'high school of the circus':

> Whilst the aim of the 'academic' rider is solely the perfection of his art, the constant preoccupation of the circus rider, who is committed to fill his employer's cash box, is to draw at all cost the applause of a crowd to which art is only of the slightest concern.

General Decarpentry and his contemporary sticklers saw equestrians who pandered to the crowds as traitors who '... roused the crowds to delirious acclamations, whilst the last survivors of the School of Versailles bowed their heads in shame.'[1] To them, any compromise at the expense of the

1 General Decarpentry, *Academic Equitation,* 1988 edition tr. Nicole Bartle (London, J.A. Allen, 1949), 3, 4.

purity of the horse's basic gaits and unforced posture was unthinkable, because it rendered dressage pointless.

General Decarpentry hoped that FEI competitions would help to preserve the classical ideals of military equitation, which relied so heavily on expert insight as to be insufficiently interesting to watch for the lay spectator. That is not how it turned out. Not in dressage, not in jumping, and not in eventing.

As has happened to other sports, the three equestrian disciplines found themselves increasingly at the mercy of a global television audience. In the 1980s, the musical freestyle was invented as an attempt to make dressage more interesting to watch. The format initially met with resistance from traditionalists, but if dressage wanted to stay in the Olympic Games in the age of professional televised sports, it had to adapt. Nobody at home in the living rooms wanted to watch athletes meticulously executing prescribed figures to technical standards beyond the audience's comprehension. Just ask the International Skating Union or the International Gymnastics Federation.

As you will know, Olympic athletes competing in subjectively scored sports originally had to document their mastery of the fundamentals of their discipline before they were allowed to move on to the more expressive freestyle events. This mastery was demonstrated in the performance of compulsory figures or routines where perfection of technique was heavily emphasised. Only those with flawless execution had a chance to shine in the finals. This ensured a certain level of excellence, but the compulsory events appealed less to audiences than the freestyle events. Because of television, the face of sport was changing.

By Atlanta 1996, the dressage musical freestyle had become an event at the Olympic Games. The equestrian equivalent of dog dancing, it is certain to have caused General Decarpentry to flip a few rotations in his grave, but it was to get much worse. As the freestyles grew more and more spectacular over the years in their attempts to wow the crowd, judges began to reward the same elements that used to be penalised in dressage because they betrayed a lack of fundamentals. Horses were increasingly tense, and their natural gaits were disrupted. Their necks were over-bent as a result of riders pulling harder on the reins to maintain control of the horses' explosive energy. Still, the scores kept climbing. The crowd loves a record-breaking score. Especially when it knows no other criterion of excellence for which to look.

Not surprisingly, the musical freestyle has since become the flagship of dressage. It is the only event within the discipline to which a TV audience can even slightly relate. It has next to nothing to do with the traditions that it claims to uphold. Singing the praises of the freestyle at the FEI Sports Forum in 2013, former FEI Director of Dressage, Trond Asmyr, unintentionally echoed General Decarpentry's criticism of 'the circus' in his enthusiastic description of what dressage had become. The freestyle was an ideal 'marketing tool' for 'reaching an audience that is lacking in dressage background' and 'increasing profitability to organisers', Asmyr boasted. In other words, FEI dressage has become the very circus at which its founding fathers scoffed. It doesn't matter in this context, whether you like the modern version of dressage better than the classical version. The discipline's profound removal from its original ideals renders it irrelevant from a historical perspective.

The other two Olympic equestrian disciplines have undergone drastic changes of their own to pay the price of the FEI's continued inclusion in the Olympic family. Athens 2004 saw the Olympic debut of the controversial short format in eventing. Riders complained at the time that this constituted a dumbing down of the discipline, but if eventing wanted to stay in the Olympics, there was no other way. As with dressage, a choice had to be made between the traditions of eventing and remaining an Olympic discipline. The FEI chose the latter.

Jumping riders are the latest to feel that their discipline has been betrayed by the FEI. The changes made to jumping in order to comply with Olympic Agenda 2020 have met with fierce opposition from the International Jumping Riders Club (IJRC), and the equestrian press has been buzzing with the very public feud between the FEI and its athletes over the rule changes made to appease the IOC.

It appears that the only equestrian tradition which has any real importance to the FEI is the tradition of remaining in the Olympic Games. This is not so strange. The FEI was founded in Lausanne in 1921 specifically to govern Olympic equestrian sport. The money the FEI receives from the IOC represents a core financing of the federation.[2] In addition, Olympic status is front and centre when it markets itself to sponsors, and further enables it to maintain a global monopoly on the disciplines under its governance.

According to the FEI General Regulations, no horse or athlete is eligible to compete in FEI or NF events within six months of having participated in 'unsanctioned events'.[3] This means that anyone who wants to organise an international equestrian competition needs the approval of the FEI and must pay the FEI to include the event in its calendar. The FEI also charges organising dues as a percentage of the prize money.[4] Should any hopeful event organisers attempt to stage a competition or a league without FEI involvement, the FEI reserves the right to label such a competition or league 'unsanctioned', which will deter athletes from taking part and risking their eligibility to compete at FEI events. The same applies to officials, who also risk a six-month quarantine by the FEI, should they

2 FEI, Report of the statutory auditor to the General Assembly on the financial statements, 2019, https://inside.fei.org/fei/about-fei/publications/fei-annual-report/2019/wp-content/uploads/2020/05/FEI-ROR-2019-with-2-signatures.pdf, accessed 19 Aug 2021.

3 FEI, General Regulations, Chapter II, Article 113.4, Jan 2021, https://inside.fei.org/sites/default/files/FEI%20General%20Regulations-effective-1Jan2021-27Nov2020-Final-Clean.pdf, accessed 19 Aug 2021.

4 FEI, Financial Charges for the year 2021, 23 Nov 2020, https://inside.fei.org/system/files/2021%20Financial%20Charges.pdf, accessed 19 Aug 2021.

participate in unsanctioned events. During the COVID-19 lockdown in early 2020, FEI judges were strictly reminded that they could be subject to disciplinary proceedings for judging online competitions via video.[5] According to the FEI, these rules exist to protect horse welfare and the integrity of the sport. But the rules have the added effect of ensuring that competing providers of equestrian sport don't nibble away at the millions of dollars in revenue the FEI takes each year from calendar fees, organising dues and media rights.

The ultimate barrier to entry for other providers of equestrian sport is Olympic affiliation. Should the FEI ever lose that, athletes and officials will have no reason to choose it over competitors. Olympic elimination will deprive the FEI of its funding, its political clout, and its monopoly. This provides one possible explanation for why successive administrators of the federation have rolled over and exposed their bellies each time the IOC has demanded reforms antithetical to the traditional values of the sport. They couldn't afford not to. No tradition is too precious to swap for four more years. When you finally decide to retire FEI events from the Olympics, you will therefore not be doing any harm to the values and traditions of classical equitation, because those have already been gouged out by the FEI in its successive scrambles to remain in the Olympics.

Equestrian traditions and modern times

Now there is just the final question: are these traditions even worthy of preservation? The point is moot because the answers to the first two questions were no and no. But let's have a look at it anyway.

5 Astrid Appels, 'FEI Judges Not Permitted to Judge Online Dressage Competitions', Eurodressage, 15 Apr 2020, https://www.eurodressage.com/2020/04/15/fei-judges-not-permitted-judge-online-dressage-competitions, accessed 19 Aug 2021.

Equestrian governing bodies are fiercely proud of the sport's military beginnings. But should they be? Equestrian sport is rooted in conflict and violence. Humans killing humans and humans killing horses. Once upon a time, we forced horses to carry us into war. Millions of them died in the First World War alone. Not one had any grudge against the other side. Not one asked to take part. Horses were simply a means to an end, sentient animals used as weapons or beasts of burden for hauling supplies and artillery to the front. When the war was over and mechanisation had ended the need for equine muscle power in the industrialised world, and we finally had a chance to let horses live their lives on their own terms, what did we do? We invented new ways to exploit and kill them, just for our amusement. The Olympic disciplines, especially dressage, commemorate the fact that, in past centuries, we involved one of the most peaceful species in the world in our own violent conflicts, forcing them to carry us to war; to starve, to be blown up and shot at and to be slaughtered and eaten when we ran out of rations. To keep that dream alive, we continue to ship horses around the world on lorries and aeroplanes, in order to make them do tricks, the purpose of which they cannot possibly comprehend. It is a truly bizarre habit, the time for which has surely passed.

Humankind stands at a crossroads regarding our relationship with each other and with the rest of the living planet. We should be looking forward to a more peaceful, reciprocally respectful coexistence. Not back in time at our own glorified violence and domination.

4

Doping, cheating, and why equestrian sport can never be clean

The IOC's commitment to protecting clean athletes and integrity in sport has been made very clear. But due to its intrinsic features, FEI-regulated equestrian sport inevitably fails to uphold the IOC's high standards.

YOU ARE THE IOC, SO I can't tell you anything you don't already know about what human athletes will do to their own bodies in order to win a medal. Now imagine that the body in question is replaceable. If and when it breaks down, another is available for purchase. The World Anti-Doping Agency (WADA) has no interest in testing this body, because it isn't human. Instead, that task has been left to an athletic federation with a vested interest in playing down the number of doping cases. What might an ambitious athlete do to such a body? History can tell us something about that.

In 2001, the Danish dressage team won the bronze at the FEI European Championships in Verden, Germany. One of the Danish horses, Jon D Pedersen's Esprit de Valdemar, was lame, so during the championships the horse was injected with adrenocorticotropic hormone (ACTH) on three separate days. ACTH was banned by the FEI's anti-doping rules, because it stimulates the production of the anti-inflammatory hormone cortisol and can therefore mask pain. The drug was not intended to turn up in Esprit de Valdemar's doping sample, and it didn't.[1]

The case only came to light because the German veterinarian who had injected Esprit de Valdemar with the banned substance sent an itemised invoice to the Danish Equestrian Federation, which was paid and subsequently leaked. This story made a big splash in the Danish press, and according to news stories at the time, the Danish Equestrian Federation considered 'handing back' the bronze medal. However, the team riders were not willing to do so, on the grounds that no team horse had failed a doping test. Technically, they were in the clear, it was felt. Several of the team members even initially refused to stop using the German veterinarian, when the Danish Equestrian Federation tried to publicly distance itself from him after the press scandal.[2]

The Danish Equestrian Federation notified the FEI that a Danish team horse had been doped at the European Championships, but to this day, the team retains its bronze medal. The veterinarian who had injected Esprit De Valdemar was a highly respected FEI vet and a former chairman of the FEI Veterinary Committee. He has functioned as a team vet or veterinary official at seven Olympic Games and a multitude of FEI championships. The year after he had injected Esprit de Valdemar with ACTH in Verden, he accompanied Italian riders as a team vet at the FEI World Equestrian Games in Jerez. In Athens 2004, he was veterinarian to the Japanese and Egyptian Olympic jumping horses.

Whether the injections administered to Esprit de Valdemar during the European Championships in 2001 were a one-off event or a regular menu item at the German veterinarian's practice is anyone's guess. Nevertheless,

1 Nynne Bjerre Christensen, 'Forbund i opløsning efter magtkamp og dopingskandale' [Federation in dissolution after power struggle and doping scandal], *Berlingske Tidende*, 23 Jun 2002.

2 Steen Ankerdal, 'VM-ryttere bruger dopinglæge' [World Championship riders use doping doctor], *B.T.*, 29 Jul 2002.

in what other Olympic sport would the international governing body knowingly and openly allow a doctor with something like that in their past to continue to ply their trade at the Olympic Games?

The laissez faire attitude displayed by the equestrian federations at the time illustrates how normalised and pervasive the creative medication of horses has historically been in FEI sport. The 2001 incident wasn't the first time the Danish Equestrian Federation had hired a foreign vet to medicate Danish team horses under dubious circumstances. In the autumn of 1993, the federation had to end its collaboration with a Belgian veterinarian after he had allegedly given unlabelled packets of mystery medication to Danish team riders who were supposed to give these drugs to their horses at home. One horse owner, who happened to also own a pharmaceutical company, had the contents of the packets analysed, and went public with the news that it had turned out to contain Warfarin—rat poison—which was thought at the time to have a therapeutic effect on navicular syndrome, a painful and debilitating condition which can arise from the wear and tear of elite jumping.[3]

The veterinarian in question—though well regarded and sought after by equestrians internationally—was not licensed to practise veterinary medicine in Denmark and would allegedly not tell riders what was in the injections their horses were also being given. This caused the chairman of the Danish Equine Veterinary Association, Dr Jørgen Falk-Rønne, to approach the Danish Equestrian Federation with suspicions that something untoward was going on. 'We thought the Equestrian Federation was being deceived, but we soon became wiser. Sports director Anne-Mette Binder told me that Danish vets were good at treating canaries and budgies, but we weren't very good at treating horses', said Dr Falk-Rønne in an interview with Danish newspaper *Berlingske Tidende* in January 1998.[4]

---

3 Nynne Bjerre Christensen and Lars Werge Andersen, 'Vennernes Forbund' [Federation of Friends], *Berlingske Tidende*, 25 Jan 1998.

4 Christensen & Andersen, 'Vennernes Forbund'.

Horse vets have told me that a similar attitude is common among equestrians, who assume that whichever veterinarian can get their lame horse going is the most highly qualified. This puts pressure on honest vets to compromise their ethics. And when the doping test comes out positive, the veterinarian is more replaceable than the rider or the coach, so often it is he or she who is made to take the blame. For some veterinarians, being thrown under the bus this way can be career-ending and life-shattering. For some others, being the fall guy appears to be part of their business model.

Sports Director Anne-Mette Binder would later say in the press that she had not known what the team horses had been given,[5] but after the Danish Equestrian Federation ended its formal relationship with the Belgian veterinarian, Danish team horses continued to be sent abroad to be treated by him with the full knowledge of the national federation.

None of this seems to have had any career-changing implications for the actors. Anne-Mette Binder is now a high-ranking FEI official and was president of the ground jury for eventing at the London Olympics in 2012. At the Tokyo Olympic Games, Binder functioned as team manager for the Danish dressage team. The Belgian veterinarian remains on the list of FEI permitted treating veterinarians, which means he can go to the Olympics as veterinarian to participating horses. He continues to be openly used by many Olympic riders, including some from Denmark. You have to look far and wide within equestrian circles to find anyone who thinks this is at all strange.

This wasn't just a Danish problem. The international equestrian scene was rife with doping scandals in the 2000s. In 2004, the FEI was having a particularly bad year. In total, 4.8 percent of doping tests were positive.[6] Four horses failed their doping tests at the Olympic Games in

5 Christensen & Andersen, 'Vennernes Forbund'.

6 Presentation by Professor Leo Jeffcott, University of Sydney, 'FEI position on anti-doping in equestrian sport', 2005, slide 28/59, https://slideplayer.com/

Athens. Two of them had won gold medals. Ireland lost its individual jumping gold when Cian O'Connor's Waterford Crystal tested positive for anti-psychotic drugs, including Fluphenazine, for which another of Mr O'Connor's horses had also tested positive in Rome a few months before the Olympic Games. The first offence had not resulted in a suspension, because Mr O'Connor had convinced the FEI that it had not been his intention to dope his horse.[7] The individual jumping gold medal in Athens went instead to Brazil's Rodrigo Pessoa, who proceeded to be disqualified from the subsequent Olympic Games, also for a prohibited substance violation.[8]

The German jumping team lost its gold medal in Athens, because Ludger Beerbaum's Goldfever tested positive for the corticosteroid Betamethasone. Mr Beerbaum has since been quoted in the German news media for saying—in the context of medicating horses—that 'anything they cannot find is allowed.'[9] He continued to represent Germany for many years after this statement, and did so in Rio 2016 as part of the bronze-medal-winning German jumping team. Mr Beerbaum has now retired from the national team, but remains heavily involved with equestrian sport. FEI Jumping Director John Roche called him 'a legend in his own lifetime', and as president of the Longines World Equestrian Academy (LWEA), Mr Beerbaum enjoys tremendous respect for his work

slide/3453820/, accessed 20 Aug 2021.

7 Grania Willis, 'Equestrian world shocked by schizophrenia drug allegations', *The Irish Times*, 3 Nov 2004, https://www.irishtimes.com/news/equestrian-world-shocked-by-schizophrenia-drug-allegations-1.1164686, accessed 20 Aug 2021.

8 Fran Jurga, 'Olympic Drug Tests: Add Pessoa to Offenders List', *Equus* Magazine, 1 Sep 2008, https://equusmagazine.com/blog-equus/olympic-drug-tests-add-pessoa-to-offenders-list, accessed 20 Aug 2021.

9 Evi Simeoni, 'Reiterliche Vereinigung suspendiert Beerbaum' [Equestrian federation suspends Beerbaum], *Frankfurter Allgemeine*, 28 May 2009, https://www.faz.net/aktuell/sport/mehr-sport/alle-spitzenkader-aufgeloest-reiterliche-vereinigung-suspendiert-beerbaum-1802635.html, accessed 20 Aug 2021.

with up-and-coming teenagers from around the world, who travel to his stables for the popular LWEA summer camps to learn the ins and outs of equestrian sport.

Ulla Salzgeber was on the Olympic gold-medal-winning dressage team for Germany in Athens, despite the fact that she had been disqualified from the World Cup final the year before, after her horse, Rusty, tested positive for testosterone. The rider's veterinarian took the blame. It seems the Swiss doctor—nicknamed 'the magician' in equestrian circles—had forgotten to tell Mrs Salzgeber and the German team coach that Rusty had been treated with the anabolic steroid. Due to Mrs Salzgeber's innocence in the matter, the FEI did not suspend the rider, but the German Equestrian Federation did. Mrs Salzgeber was given a very short competition ban—two months—just short enough to allow her to qualify for the Olympics.[10]

Despite this unfortunate blunder and a few others like it, the Swiss veterinarian continued to enjoy an illustrious career in equestrian sport with several Olympic riders among his clients.

The normalisation of drugs that enhance performance

One problem with equestrian sport is that horses are frequently injured and sick and are medicated all the time between competitions. A performance horse may be sedated for various routine procedures (such as clipping, mane pulling, shoeing, and transportation) which they find aversive or frightening. Diseased joints are injected with local anaesthetics for diagnostic procedures and corticosteroids for therapeutic or palliative purposes. Non-steroidal anti-inflammatory drugs are used to manage colic, muscle stiffness, hoof abscesses, and many other conditions. To

10 Astrid Appels, 'Two Months Suspension for Ulla Salzgeber', Eurodressage, 6 Feb 2004, https://www.eurodressage.com/2004/02/06/two-months-suspension-ulla-salzgeber, accessed 20 Aug 2021.

riders who were used to riding medicated horses at home and considered medication a normal part of everyday horse management, it seemed unfair that using drugs at a competition could result in being labelled a doper and horse abuser.

The FEI, on its part, was struggling with its public image after Athens 2004, and badly needed to reduce the number of positive doping cases in the sport. At the time, 90 percent of FEI doping cases involved substances which acted on the horse's musculoskeletal system. This is not surprising, because it has since been documented by several scientific studies that a lot of competition horses are unsound.[11] In 2004, 84 percent of FEI doping cases involved one of three drug types; non-steroid anti-inflammatory (NSAID), sedative, and corticosteroid. NSAIDs and corticosteroids alleviate the pain and inflammation which cause a horse to be lame.[12] Sedatives can mitigate the symptoms of anxiety which can arise when a horse is forced to perform despite being in pain.

The solution to the problem was to re-define 'doping'. In April 2005, the FEI issued a press release stating that the kinds of drugs that—until then—had caused the vast majority of doping cases in the sport would no longer be referred to as doping agents.[13] Since the steroids injected into diseased joints, the sedatives needed to settle the anxiety of frightened horses, and the NSAIDs routinely used to mask general discomfort were all part of normal life on the farm, these drugs became reclassified as 'medication', defined by the FEI as 'agents which could influence

11 HorseTalk staff writer, 'Repeated studies show shortcomings among riders in identifying lameness in horses', HorseTalk, 26 Mar 2017, https://www.horsetalk.co.nz/2017/03/26/shortcomings-riders-lameness-horses/#axzz4ccOEeQhE, accessed 20 Aug 2021.

12 Earl Gaughan, D.V.M., Dipl. ACVS, 'Pain Recognition and Management in Horses', Merck Animal Health, 2018, https://www.merck-animal-health-equine.com/news/article/34, accessed 20 Aug 2021.

13 FEI, 'FEI General Assembly: Task Force on Anti Doping and Medication Policy', 9 Apr 2005, https://inside.fei.org/media-updates/fei-general-assembly-task-force-anti-doping-and-medication-policy, accessed 20 Aug 2021.

performance by relieving pain, sedating, stimulating or producing/modifying other physiological or behavioural effects.'

The most interesting word in this definition is the word 'could'. These drugs absolutely do influence performance, and it is easy to understand why. In equestrian sport, horses are controlled by riders mainly via what is known as negative reinforcement. An aversive stimulus is applied—this could be the poke of a spur or a pull on the reins—and the horse performs whichever behaviour they have learned to perform in order to make the discomfort cease. The rider then removes or softens the aversive influence on the horse as 'payment' for a desired behaviour.

Just like humans, horses may get sore and stiff from putting in a hard physical effort. Anyone who has ever been sore after a workout knows that even normal and harmless post-exercise soreness can be quite painful and significantly affect range of motion. In a horse, this pain competes with the aversiveness of the rider's commands with the spurs, whip, and reins, making it more likely that the horse refuses or resists the rider's requests. In cases where no painless choice is available to the horse, anxiety arises and the horse may try to defend themselves against the rider by bucking, rearing or bolting. Just as we saw Saint Boy (the horse at the centre of the modern pentathlon scandal) do in Tokyo.

A rider's athletic performance is largely determined by their ability to control their horse, and so any drug which renders a horse more compliant will affect the rider's performance. The drug doesn't have to make the horse any faster or stronger than they normally are. In equestrian sport, drugs can enhance performance simply by making the horse less unwilling to do as they are told. This is automatically achieved when any kind of pain killer is used to alleviate any kind of stiffness or inflammation.

NSAIDs are not considered performance enhancing when taken by human athletes because the human athlete is both the one who wants to win and the one whose body has to work through the pain. In Equestrian, the athlete wants to win and the horse wants to be elsewhere, doing horse things with other horses. Part of the performance of the rider is to transform these divergent points of view into obedience on the horse's part. That is why the use of pain medication in horse sport will never be equivalent to the use of pain medication in sports where only humans are involved.

It has been argued that allowing certain medications to be used in horse sport provides just as level a playing field as a zero tolerance to drugs. But another difference between a human athlete and a horse is that a human athlete can give their informed consent to the treatment. The human athlete is making a decision about their own body, based on what they know about their condition. A horse does not know why they ache, cannot assess the degree of risk involved, and has no agency over whether or not they are medicated. Horses can and do have catastrophic breakdowns and end up dead or permanently disabled when they are made to compete on analgesic drugs. But the FEI's redefinition of doping in 2005 now allowed the use of many such drugs, previously defined as doping agents, to be swept under the carpet as cases of 'medication'.

In Hong Kong (Beijing Olympics), things went from bad to worse, despite the FEI's new and exclusive definition of doping. Five jumping horses failed their tests and were disqualified from the Olympic Games. Norway lost its team bronze in jumping when Tony André Hansen's Camiro tested positive for capsaicin.

Capsaicin caused all but one adverse analytical finding in Equestrian at the 2008 Olympic Games. It is the compound which gives chili peppers their heat, and works by causing a sensation of burning and pain to the skin that can last for hours. Capsaicin is banned by the FEI because riders have applied it to horses' legs to make them more sensitive to pain. The pain is intended to render horses more 'careful', as riders call it when a horse appears to try their best not to knock down obstacles. In the past, this effect has been achieved by putting sharp objects inside the boots on the horse's legs, eventually forcing officials at horse shows to start performing boot and bandage checks.

Capsaicin plays the role of an invisible thumb tack, causing pain to the horse when they (or the rider) make a mistake and hit a rail. Usually, riders caught using this drug have claimed that they were applying it to the skin in order to provide pain relief (the affected area eventually goes somewhat numb), but as the analgesic properties of the substance are debatable, such claims may also be viewed as attempts to downgrade a case of doping and horse abuse to a 'controlled medication violation'. One case brought before the Court of Arbitration for Sport after the 2008 Olympic Games resulted in the following statement from the Court as to whether the use of capsaicin is a doping or a medication violation: 'In the Panel's view, the fact that capsaicin is also a pain-reliever does not and cannot elude the fact that it is indeed an "agent used to hypersensitise or desensitise the limbs or body parts", thus to be considered as a doping substance.'[14]

When so many riders were disqualified for abusing the same substance in Hong Kong, it was likely because they had not reckoned with the sophistication of the laboratories of the Hong Kong Jockey Club. European laboratories were unable to detect the presence of capsaicin in a horse's system at the time; the Hong Kong Jockey Club's laboratory was not. Norwegian FEI veterinarian Dr Svein Bakke said at the time that he would not be surprised if 30 percent of jumping horses competing in the 2008 Olympic Games had capsaicin in their systems. 'When 30 percent of horses tested during the Olympic Games tested positive for capsaicin, that is reason to believe that 30 percent of the horses who were not tested were also [under the influence] of

14 Court of Arbitration for Sport, CAS 2008/A/1700 Deutsche Reiterliche Vereinigung e. V. v/FEI & Christian Ahlmann CAS 2008/A/1710 Christian Ahlmann v/FEI, 30 Apr 2009, p. 19, para 89, https://arbitrationlaw.com/sites/default/files/free_pdfs/CAS%202008-A-1700%20DRV%20v%20FEI%20%26%20CA%20%26%20CAS%202008-A-1710%20CA%20v%20FEI%20Award.pdf, accessed 20 Aug 2021.

this drug,' Dr Bakke said at a Norwegian press conference following the disqualification of Tony André Hansen. 'When I am at horse shows abroad and we search the waste bins in the stables, I have yet to fail to find spent tubes containing this drug. But we have never found those who have used it because European laboratories are so far unable to show the presence of capsaicin in blood or urine samples.'[15]

One Olympic dressage horse tested positive for the NSAID Felbinac in Hong Kong, but thanks to the new definition of doping, this was merely a case of 'medication'.[16]

The scandals in Hong Kong left equestrian sport in crisis. The FEI announced that what was needed was to make the anti-doping rules even clearer by publishing an exhaustive list of all the drugs that were not allowed—doping agents as well as 'medications'. Hitherto, the FEI had published categories of prohibited substances according to their effect, but there was nowhere for riders to look up specific drugs to see how they were classed.

The result was the FEI's 'progressive prohibited list', which was voted through by secret ballot at the 2009 General Assembly in Copenhagen.[17] The name of the list may amuse some readers when they learn that NSAIDs had been banned by the FEI since 1993, and horses would now once again—according to the list—be allowed to compete on non-steroidal anti-inflammatory drugs such as phenylbutazone (colloquially known as 'bute'), which mask pain and inflammation. In fact, the FEI had generously increased the maximum permitted

15 Knut Houge, 'Han punkterte advokatens forsvarstale' [He punctured the lawyer's defense speech], Hest Norge, 28 Jun 2010, https://www.hest.no/article.html?news.nid=5129, accessed 20 Aug 2021.

16 FEI, Decision in the Positive Medication Case involving the horse MYTHILUS, 21 Sep 2008, https://inside.fei.org/media-updates/decision-positive-medication-case-involving-horse-mythilus, accessed 20 Aug 2021.

17 FEI, 'FEI General Assembly Votes for New Anti-Doping Measures', press release, 19 Nov 2009, https://dressage-news.com/2009/11/19/fei-general-assembly-votes-for-new-ant-doping-measures, accessed 20 Aug 2021.

concentration of bute in a horse's blood by 300 percent since the initial ban in 1993. Progressive!

The method by which the FEI managed to get the progressive list voted through was the subject of some controversy. A month before the vote, delegates had been sent a list, according to which there were—as expected—no maximum permitted levels for NSAIDs such as phenylbutazone and flunixin. They were simply prohibited as they had been for 16 years. However, a few days before the General Assembly was to kick off, the original list was joined by its progressive counterpart. Now there were two lists to vote on. Which one would go through? Delegates were emailed notice of the addition, but many were already in transit to Copenhagen, and there were reports of chaotic scenes as national federation representatives (many of them from countries considered 'non-riding' by Count Breido zu Rantzau) attempted upon their arrival to make sense of the situation.[18]

After the vote, as the implications of the result dawned on delegates, panic ensued. The European federations were outraged. The image of the sport would be ruined. People would think this change had been made to reduce the number of positive doping tests without reducing the doping. FEI vice president Sven Holmberg said the vote had 'cut the legs off the clean sports campaign'.[19] Sponsors wouldn't buy it. The IOC would be appalled. In countries like Denmark, France and Sweden, drugging horses to enable them to take part in competitions was illegal. In the end, the FEI was forced to delay the implementation of the progressive list.

In 2010, the FEI NSAIDs Congress was held to give stakeholders a chance to hear each other out. On the one hand, it was felt that horses

18 Neil Clarkson, 'The drugs vote that rained on the FEI's parade', HorseTalk, 17 Dec 2009, https://www.horsetalk.co.nz/features/feihorsedoping-174.shtml, accessed 20 Aug 2021.

19 Pippa Cuckson, 'Shocking Vote Legalizes Bute In FEI Competition,' *Chronicle of the Horse*, 20 Nov 2009, https://www.chronofhorse.com/article/shocking-vote-legalizes-bute-fei-competition, accessed 20 Aug 2021.

need medication to cope with the physical burden and mental stress of competition life. The lifestyle and workload of an international performance horse can often lead to their needing treatment for respiratory, gastrointestinal, psychological, and musculoskeletal problems. Some stakeholders did not consider it fair on the horse to withhold treatment for such problems in order to be able to compete. A high-profile proponent of this point of view was legendary Belgian veterinarian, Dr Leo De Backer, who has been a treating veterinarian at six Olympic Games. He said that, given the inevitability that some horses are going to be medicated when they compete, comparatively safe drugs like bute should be de-regulated in order to prevent the illicit use of more hazardous ones. Dr De Backer pointed out to delegates at the congress that zero tolerance did not equate to zero doping:

> Everybody here knows, because we are not so naive, that there are still several drugs that are undetectable. To mention one name that is very unhealthy for horses: ACTH. It has been used for horses for many years. Even today, a lot of horses get an unhealthy drug like ACTH.[20]

Clean or corrupt, international horse sport and welfare don't mix

In any other sport, such candid statements to confirm the existence of a normalised doping culture during a conference might cause gasps of horror. But that day in 2010, at the Olympic Museum in Lausanne, Dr De Backer wasn't saying anything the other delegates did not already know. Unless the physical and mental demands on horses were significantly reduced, the notion of drug free equestrian sport would be utopian.

20 FEI NSAID Congress Question and Answer Session, YouTube video published 1 Sep 2010, timecode 47:49, https://www.youtube.com/watch?v=kCP707F70Vc&t=2923s, accessed 20 Aug 2021.

'*Citius, Altius, Fortius*': 'Faster, Higher, Stronger'. FEI sport lives up to the Olympic motto at the expense of the animals whose welfare the federation claims to place above all else.

United States team vet, Dr Tim Ober, chimed in during the Q&A at the NSAIDs congress to elucidate the challenges that face veterinarians in elite showjumping. He explained that there was very little that could be done for a sore or injured horse during international competitions if doping and medication rules were to be respected. In the span of eight weeks, horses had to get to twelve Nations Cup competitions, three of which were back-to-back. This meant horses spending two days in transit directly after a major event, arriving at the next show just in time for the veterinary check. Dr Ober asked:

> They had jumped the Nations Cup, two rounds, on Friday and they had jumped the Grand Prix on Sunday. Then they had got on a truck, and, in the case of Rome to St Gallen, been shipped for two days to arrive in St Gallen and then [attend the veterinary check] again, I believe it was Wednesday in the afternoon. That's quite a schedule, and to practically expect a horse to go through that without support, without help, I think that is rather unreasonable and I question in all seriousness whether that is in the best interest of the horse, so how do we handle these situations?[21]

In other words, international sport horses will suffer without drugs. But they may also suffer with drugs, as pointed out by Swedish Equestrian Federation consultant veterinarian, Dr Peter Kallings. At the NSAIDs congress, he was one of the people who suggested that the answer to the FEI's doping problem was not to allow drugs but to reduce the demands placed on the horses. He called it bad management to put horses under such pressure that they could only function if medicated. He also pointed out that to allow horses to be on NSAIDs at FEI events would render

21 FEI NSAID Congress Q & A, timecode 5:01.

the pre-competition veterinary checks pointless. It may not surprise you that I agree with Dr Kallings. What does it say about a sport that its 'athletes' can only cope with life if they are full of drugs? How does that fit with Olympic values?

Brazil's Rodrigo Pessoa, Olympic individual jumping gold medallist, suggested that riders could simply avoid riding in France and Sweden, where the legislation would not allow for the implementation of the progressive list. 'We go to the rest of the world. We go to new places where we can do our work and take care of our horses.' Mr Pessoa also said that, alternatively, he would be happy to ride in fewer competitions.[22]

It is typical of the prevalent discourse in equestrian circles that both Dr Ober and Mr Pessoa use terms like 'support', 'help', and 'take care of' when they are talking about using drugs to mask symptoms of over-training and suboptimal husbandry. The shared values inside the international equestrian community are at times in stark contrast with those of the general public. This was true in 2010 and is even more so today.

In the end, the FEI was forced by public outrage to abandon the progressive list and removed most NSAID thresholds from its list of prohibited substances. An exception was made for salicylic acid (a metabolite of aspirin), which must be allowed a threshold because it can be found in plants commonly ingested by horses, such as lucerne hay. The progressive list had raised the threshold for salicylic acid, and the new threshold was kept in the final list. This was a controversial decision, because the FEI had originally lowered its threshold for salicylic acid in 1999 based on evidence that the substance was being abused.[23]

According to a letter sent to FEI President Princess Haya in November 2009 (after the progressive list had first been voted through) by former

22 FEI NSAID Congress Q & A, timecode 43:07.

23 Professor Leo Jeffcott and colleagues, 'Letter from FEI Vets to Princess Haya Against Bute', Eventing Nation, Nov 2009, https://eventingnation.com/letter-from-fei-vets-against-fei-ruling/, accessed 20 Aug 2021.

chair of the FEI Veterinary Committee, Professor Leo Jeffcott, riders in the 1990s were gaming the higher threshold for salicylic acid to enhance the performance of their horses: 'Salicylic acid had been found in CORAL COVE at the 1998 World Equestrian Games, and it was apparent at the time that intravenous "topping up" to the threshold was not a rare occurrence,' stated the letter, which was co-signed by 14 other veterinarians of international repute—including the former chair of the FEI's Medication Advisory Group, Dr Andrew Higgins. The letter went on to cite the scientific basis for lowering the thresholds:

> After analysis of 650 equine urine samples collected worldwide and considerable discussion it was decided to reduce the FEI threshold to below that used by racing (where there was no evidence of similar abuse). The work was reported to the International Conference of Racing Analysts and Veterinarians in 2004 and was subsequently published. There was therefore a clear rationale for the threshold of 625 µg/ml in urine or 5.4 µg/ml in plasma.[24]

The FEI did not heed the warning and decided to go ahead with the higher threshold. According to the 2020 FEI Equine Prohibited Substances list, the threshold for salicylic acid remains at the level Professor Jeffcott and his colleagues warned against: 750 micrograms per millilitre in urine and 6.5 micrograms per millilitre in plasma. As recently as 2017, researchers from the Universities of Hannover and Cologne looked into the FEI's current salicylic acid thresholds and, based on their results, warned that the thresholds were set too high to prevent misuse of the drug.[25]

Here is the thing about the FEI Prohibited Substances List. In addition to salicylic acid, it contains quite a few other performance-enhancing

24 Jeffcott and colleagues, 'Letter'.

25 Kathrin Buntenkötter, 'Pharmacokinetics and in vitro efficacy of salicylic acid after oral administration of acetylsalicylic acid in horses,' *BMC Veterinary Research*, 13/28 (2016), https://www.ncbi.nlm.nih.gov/pmc/articles/PMC5247822/, accessed 20 Aug 2021. doi: 10.1186/s12917-017-0955-1

drugs which are not actually banned, because the FEI uses the term 'Prohibited Substances' as an umbrella term for banned substances and controlled medication substances, so that saying that a substance is prohibited does not automatically indicate that it is banned. If this baffles you, don't worry. You are meant to be confused.

Reading through the disciplinary cases from the 2008 Olympic Games, I came across analytical findings I had never heard of before. One horse tested positive for two other drugs besides capsaicin, including one local anaesthetic, mepivacaine. However, most people will not have heard of this, because the treatment with the local anaesthetic—despite it being listed by the FEI as a prohibited substance—had been authorised by the FEI Veterinary Commission on the day of the Olympic team finals in jumping.[26]

The CAS papers make no mention of whether the local anaesthetic was administered in connection with the chronic back pain from which the horse had been suffering for months according to the testimony of his rider. Nor does this matter. What matters is that a rider can now apply for permission to treat their horse with prohibited substances (formerly known as doping agents) during an FEI competition. Should the horse be selected for testing, and the drugs be detected by the laboratory, no anti-doping or controlled medication case will arise.

The decision to allow a horse in need of 'emergency medical treatment' to be given drugs, declared 'fit for fight', and continue to compete in the Olympic Games is not made by WADA. It is made within a closed loop of FEI veterinarians and officials. The veterinary officials who must approve the applications filled in by treating veterinarians for the medicating of horses with prohibited substances during an event are plucked from the pool of FEI treating veterinarians, which means the two groups overlap. Veterinary officials at Olympic Games also need to make a day-to-day living, and their ability to do so often relies on cultivating professional relationships with the very riders who may also rely on them at a major

26 Court of Arbitration for Sport, CAS 2008/A/1700.

event for permission to medicate their horse with a prohibited substance. Such a system is a petri dish for conflicts of interest.

Whilst it has always been possible for horses to get emergency treatment during events, the prohibited list finally decided upon in 2010 served as a catalogue of which drugs to apply to use and which drugs were completely off limits. With the right veterinarian and the right paperwork, why would a rider even need to cheat?

On the list of controlled medication substances for 2020 are several beta blockers, sedatives, NSAIDs, and glucocorticoids. Even ACTH has been un-banned, so that it now appears on the list of controlled medication substances. How often you think any of these drugs, formerly known as doping substances, are authorised by the FEI for use during competition depends entirely on the thickness of your tin foil hat. But when Dr Jan Greve—Dutch team veterinarian for four decades—retired in 2018, he gave a frank interview to *The Horse* magazine. Asked what he was most proud of in his career, Dr Greve said that it was the fact that no horse in his care had ever failed a doping test. He admitted that he had done 'necessary' things that were not allowed, but it had never resulted in a positive test. 'The new regulations after Hong Kong made it all easier,' said the veteran FEI veterinarian to the Australian publication. 'In the past everything had to be sneaky. Ludger's law was: "Anything they cannot find is allowed". Now much more is allowed, provided that we request it in advance.'[27]

An example of this is Betamethasone—the corticosteroid which cost Mr Beerbaum and the rest of the German team their Olympic gold medal in 2004. It is among the substances no longer considered doping agents by the FEI. Horses can now compete on this drug as long as the FEI has approved its use.

---

27 Jacob Melissen, 'Dutch Vet – Jan Greve – An explosive interview', *The Horse* magazine, 23 Feb 2018, https://www.horsemagazine.com/thm/2018/02/dutch-vet-jan-greve-an-explosive-interview/, accessed 20 Aug 2021.

Even without the necessary paperwork, athletes caught riding horses with prohibited substances in their systems receive much more lenient punishments if the substance is a controlled medication than if it is outright banned. In Dubai in 2019, a Uruguayan endurance horse tested positive for a corticosteroid which had been injected directly into the mare's arthritic fetlock joint six days before a 160-kilometre endurance race. The horse's rider was an FEI veterinarian, who had also been the one to inject the horse with the steroid hormone. She received an eight-month suspension—but only because it was the second time she had been caught using the same drug on the same horse before a competition. Otherwise, the FEI would have suspended her for only four months, according to the published decision by the FEI Tribunal. Despite the repeat offence, the veterinarian was found by the FEI to bear no significant fault, after she had 'established on a balance of probabilities' how the prohibited substance entered her horse's system, which was easy to do since she was the one who had injected the steroid hormone into the horse's diseased joint.[28] The FEI Tribunal did not question the veterinarian's decision to race a chronically lame horse 160 kilometres through the desert. Nor did the FEI remove the person responsible from the list of FEI permitted treating veterinarians.[29]

At the London 2012 Olympics, one jumping medallist had been caught riding a horse with two NSAIDs in their system just six months earlier. He could not explain to the FEI Tribunal or the Court of Arbitration for Sport how the substances entered his horse. The rider (although he had a previous doping offence on record) eventually got away with only two months' suspension, allowing him to compete and

28 Decision of the FEI Tribunal, Case: 2019/CM04, 22 Apr 2020, https://inside.fei.org/system/files/Case_2019-CM04-LOBITA-Final_Tribunal_Decision-Approval_of_Agreement_between_Parties-22_April_2020.pdf, accessed 20 Aug 2021.

29 FEI, FEI Permitted Treating Veterinarians, 103, https://data.fei.org/OffListRpts/OfficialsByAddRole_TV.pdf, accessed 20 Aug 2021.

win a medal at the Olympic Games, because his 2012 incident was not a 'doping offence', but merely a 'controlled medication violation'.[30]

Even with the generous loopholes offered by the distinction between 'banned substances' and 'controlled medication', horses are still failing their doping tests. In the first quarter of 2021, the FEI Tribunal made decisions in two cases of horses who had been given anabolic steroids ahead of competitions.[31] In both cases, the rider claimed not to have known that they were riding a horse who was on anabolic steroids. In both cases, the rider's defence was that the horse's owner had doped the horse without their knowledge. And in both cases, the FEI Tribunal accepted that the rider bore no significant fault or negligence for the rule violation. This seems surprising since the samples from both horses contained the anabolic steroid Boldenone, classed by the FEI as a 'banned substance'. According to the FEI Clean Sport website, 'banned substances' are 'substances that are deemed by the FEI to have no legitimate use in the competition horse and/or have a high potential for abuse'. Whether the riders in these cases were telling the truth or not, the decisions highlight a significant problem regarding horse sport. As long as there is someone else willing to say they injected the horse with anabolic steroids, the rider can simply claim ignorance. This is hardly a sound basis for a credible anti-doping programme.

---

30 Court of Arbitration for Sport, CAS 2012/A/2808 Abdullah Waleed Sharbatly v. Fédération Equestre Internationale, 17 Jul 2021, 4, https://inside.fei.org/system/files/LOBSTER%20-%20CAS%20Final%20Decision%20-%2017%20July%202012.pdf, accessed 20 Aug 2021.

31 Decision of the FEI Tribunal: Case number: FEI 2020/BS07 – EASY BOY 23, 7 Apr 2021, https://inside.fei.org/system/files/20210407_Final%20Decision%20 2020-BS07%20EASY%20BOY%2023%20-%20C21-0011%20-%20ALBISU.pdf, accessed 5 Sep 2021; and Decision of the FEI Tribunal: Case number: FEI 2020/BS04 – GUCCI, 25 Jan 2021. https://inside.fei.org/system/files/20210125_Final%20Decision%20C21-0002%20-%20%202020%20 BS04%20GUCCI.pdf, accessed 5 Sep 2021.

Additional difficulties in avoiding prohibited substances in horses

Horses did not evolve to live in crates; travel puts them at risk of pneumonia and life-threatening diarrhoea, and equestrian training is stressful and sometimes painful for them. They may develop gastric ulcers, shipping fever, phobias, hypersensitivity to dust, and aching joints, all of which can be at least partially alleviated by the use of prohibited substances. This is another example of the unsolvable paradoxes faced by the FEI. This particular paradox gets even more unsolvable when you consider the risk of contamination. A positive doping test in any sport is typically followed by the athlete claiming it happened by accident. Equestrians are the same. It is always down to some groom who touched a rake that had been transported on a bus where the driver's cat used to party with Keith Richards. But in horse sport, stories of contamination are far more likely to be true. No rider can be with their horse all the time or be completely in control of what goes into that horse's body. Even if they could, what kind of life would that be for a horse?

Horses evolved to graze and browse for at least sixteen hours per day. They are meant to be outside with other horses, munching on herbs and hedges. Even competition horses, who are often confined to the stable, eat hay and grain which can contain any number of compounds on the prohibited list. Horses don't know or care about contamination. They may lick the resident dog or accept a treat from a passing stranger. To place a horse in a situation where they can't possibly ingest or otherwise come into contact with a contaminant is to place that horse in a prison.

The FEI publishes a guide for riders to help them avoid contamination. It states that poppies, crocuses, nightshade or lupins growing nearby can cause a positive test for controlled medication. The same goes for coffee. Large areas of the planet are basically unsuitable for FEI horses on this basis alone.

When Dr Roly Owers advises FEI stakeholders on how to maintain a social licence to operate, he tells them that it is imperative that they are seen to provide their horses with access to the three Fs: Friends, Freedom and Forage. The kind of box in which competition horses are typically kept is essentially a fancy cage; and caged animals are going out of style.

Horses are social animals, and although the norm for FEI horses is still to keep them in individual boxes, they really need to belong to a bonded family group and live in herds in free-range systems, like other social animals. This is unavoidably incompatible with horse sport, because competition horses are frequently bought and sold and also spend a lot of time away from home. Elite jumping horses are more or less permanently on the road. Herd life involves further risk of contamination, because some prohibited substances can be excreted in urine and faeces and later be reabsorbed by another horse.

Urine from humans has also been alleged to cause contamination. In 2020, the FEI reversed its suspension of a Swiss jumping rider because it could not be ruled out that her horse had accidentally ingested the banned substance Tramadol by eating contaminated hay. The Court of Arbitration for Sport heard that the contamination might have been caused by a member of the rider's support staff having urinated in the horse lorry and possibly in other places close to the horse, after having taken an opioid analgesic for his back pain.

The FEI knows that going forward, riders will have to demonstrate that their horses are housed and handled in a more species-appropriate way than they currently are. This means giving horses the freedom to go outside whenever they want to. They have to be allowed to eat the plants they can find, and they have to be allowed to interact with other horses and their environment in general. Most horses are curious, gregarious creatures who like to know what is going on around them. If allowed, they wander and investigate, and they prefer to do so as a group. That is never going to work with the strict liability principle imposed by WADA norms. As far as clean sport is concerned, horses are a square peg and the modern Olympic Games are a round hole.

The equestrian disciplines at the London, Rio, and Tokyo Olympics were clean by the FEI's standards. Such achievements should, however, be viewed in the context of the ever-shifting goalpost which is called, in its current form, the FEI Equine Anti-Doping and Controlled Medication Regulations. In any case, the significance of 'clean' championships begins to fade as soon as you become aware of the FEI's deregulation of performance-enhancing surgery during the past decade. In this time, the FEI has allowed horses to compete after having operations to mask the symptoms of chronic injuries. The cases of two horses, called Anton and Never, exemplify how.

5

The stories of Anton and Never

To 'encourage and support measures relating to the medical care and health of athletes' is an important part of the IOC's mission.[1] *But there is nothing healthy about tricking a chronically injured 'athlete' into loading a damaged limb. To eke out the final dregs of profit from their assets, owners of sick horses may pay veterinarians to perform surgery, which renders the horse unable to feel that they are injured. Thanks to the FEI's deregulation of this practice in recent years, there is now very little to stop it from happening.*

ANTON 515 WAS AN EIGHT-YEAR-OLD FEI jumping horse who was in a lot of pain in the summer and autumn of 2012. Bursitis and debilitating lesions to the cartilage and tendons in his right front foot made him unable to perform in the jumping arena anymore. From the outside, a horse's hoof looks tough, but inside its capsule (composed of hard keratin) are tiny bones, connective tissues and intricate vascular structures which provide shock absorption through a mechanism similar to hydraulics. Once these tissues are damaged, they are notoriously difficult to heal. Anton's condition was chronic. According to the gelding's medical

1 IOC, Olympic Charter, 17 Jul 2020, chapter 2.10, https://stillmed.olympics.com/media/Document%20Library/OlympicOrg/General/EN-Olympic-Charter.pdf?_ga=2.254022350.73135699.1630760712-1999677687.1629286348, accessed 5 Sep 2021.

journal, he was unlikely to recover from his injuries. His prognosis was described as 'poor'.

In such cases, there is something the veterinarian can do to make a horse like Anton comfortable, apart from giving him drugs. The nerve to the site of injury can be cut, which, in Anton's case, would stop his foot from sending pain signals to his brain. He would feel as if the injuries didn't exist. In October 2012, Anton underwent this surgery on both his front limbs.

As you can imagine, making a horse permanently unable to feel his injuries comes with a risk of those injuries becoming worse, or of fresh trauma going unnoticed. Pain has a function, which is to warn the animal who feels it against loading the injured limb. Presumably, this is why—up until 2013—the FEI Veterinary Regulations included a very clear ban on riding horses who had undergone this type of surgery: 'Horses may not compete with a tracheotomy (i.e., a surgical opening through the skin into the trachea) or after a neurectomy has been carried out.'[2]

This rule was quite clear. Neurectomies are used as a last resort to mask pain from chronic injuries, so any horse who has undergone this surgery is most likely to be injured for the rest of their life. The surgery itself is performance enhancing in that it enables a horse to perform, who would not otherwise be able to do so. If a rider were to have their veterinarian inject a horse with a drug which had the same effect as that of the neurectomy, it would be a clear case of doping. (Well, maybe not: the FEI would call it a 'controlled medication case'.)

The surgeon who performed Anton's neurectomies (an equine vet of international renown) was kind enough to send me a copy of the

2 FEI Veterinary Regulations, 12th edition, 2010, page 22, Article 1011 2.6.4. Veterinary Examinations and Horse Inspections, https://equestrianorganizers.com/uploads_nieuws/documenten/2009-12-21-11:56:12_FEI%20Veterinary%20Regulations%2012th%20edition-in%20force%20on%205April10.pdf, accessed 20 Aug 2021.

standard guidelines that are given to horse owners when their horses are discharged after having the surgery. I have translated them from Danish into English:

> [Horse's name] is hereby discharged after neurectomy to [left/right] front leg. The operation has been performed [date] and went according to plan. The purpose of the operation is to remove chronic pain in the back part of the hoof on [left/right] front leg, which it has not been possible to cure with medical treatment.[3]

Then there are some instructions on after care. And then this:

> It is brought to your attention that the horse's ability to feel pain in the back part of the hoof is non-existent, for which reason it is of the utmost importance to check the hooves daily and palpate the legs for any swelling or heat. If doubts arise, the horse's regular veterinarian must be called at once. We also direct your attention to the fact that horses who have undergone neurectomy may not be trained for or participate in competitions.[4]

Removal of the ban on de-nerved horses in competition

That last part about the horse being ineligible for competition now refers only to Danish law, not FEI rules. In 2013, the FEI Veterinary Regulations had a major overhaul. Among the changes made was a removal of the ban on riding de-nerved horses.[5] In 2017, when Anton's story was first published, I asked the FEI why it had done this, but the question was sidestepped.

3 Højgård Hestehospital [Højgård Horse Hospital] patient guidelines provided by email to author, 22 May 2017.

4 Ibid.

5 FEI, 2014 Veterinary Regulations, 13th edition, 1 Jan 2014, p 49, Article 1034 paragraph 2, https://www.dierenkliniekecht.nl/sites/default/files/documenten/FEI_Veterinary_Regulations_2014.pdf, accessed 21 Aug 2021.

Instead, the FEI communications department repeatedly referred to the changes in the Veterinary Regulations regarding neurectomy:

> Horses are not eligible to compete when a limb, or part of a limb, is hyposensitive or hypersensitive (both of which shall constitute 'abnormal limb sensitivity'). Hypersensitive limbs have an excessive or abnormal reaction to palpation. Hyposensitive limbs include any alteration in sensitivity induced by a neurectomy or chemical desensitisation for as long as the alteration in sensitivity persists.

'For as long as the alteration in sensitivity persists' in relation to neurectomy refers to the ability of nerves to regenerate. A chronically injured horse may have to have several neurectomies in their life in order to stay comfortable enough to enjoy their retirement. The nerves re-grow, the horse becomes lame again and the procedure is repeated. But why would the FEI need to change its rules to allow de-nerved horses to compete again after their nerves regenerate? A chronically injured horse will be as lame as before they had the surgery. They will have no business competing at an FEI event.

The only imaginable reason for deregulation is the allowance for a hypothetical scenario where a sport horse is so badly injured and so unlikely to recover, that palliative care is deemed to be the only humane option left (besides euthanasia) and the horse is de-nerved, because even standing in the field eating grass is going to be too painful for the rest of their life. In this hypothetical scenario, that horse's nerves then regenerate completely, so that there is no alteration in sensation whatsoever. At the same time, the career-ending injuries, which originally caused both veterinarian and horse owner to throw in the towel, miraculously disappear. In such a case, the horse would be eligible to compete at FEI events once again. This is an unlikely scenario. And whereas the old rule regarding neurectomy was clear, the new one is impossible to enforce.

The problem is that there is no reliable test to determine whether a past neurectomy is still affecting a horse. Once upon a time, a de-nerved horse would have had scars and obvious issues with proprioception. However, modern veterinary surgery is so advanced that nerves can be cut precisely to affect the targeted area, while normal sensitivity is retained in adjacent areas. The skin prick tests used by the FEI, when testing for abnormal limb sensitivity, were not appropriate in this context. When the FEI first confirmed that it had begun to allow horses to compete post-neurectomy, the communications department also told me that this was contingent on the individual horse having regained normal sensitivity in the limb, and that 'The FEI is currently working with veterinary specialists to develop a method to objectively measure sensitivity in horses—should horses not have normal sensitivity, they would not be able to compete.'[6]

This means that since 2013, the FEI has been allowing de-nerved horses to compete, on the condition that their limb sensitivity is no longer affected by the neurectomy, while at the same time, it has still not developed a method to objectively determine that this is the case. For none of this time has a method existed by which show veterinarians and officials can evaluate whether a past neurectomy is still affecting a horse. This puts the discussion about aspirin firmly into perspective.

The FEI had effectively de-regulated performance-enhancing surgery in horse sport. The take-home message for riders was that de-nerved horses could now be ridden at FEI competitions, and this would likely have been regarded as good news, because a lot of sport horses are unsound, and having the veterinarian perform a neurectomy is a way to make the lameness go away without risking a medication or doping case.

Less than six months after Anton had been discharged from the equine hospital following his neurectomies, he competed at FEI competitions in Arezzo, Tuscany, obediently jumping the obstacles and landing on his

6 Email from FEI Communications Department to author, 17 May 2017.

shattered foot because he could not feel the damage it was doing. No FEI check caught this.

Shortly before his 9th birthday, Anton jumped in his final show. After that, he went back to the clinic. He had an MRI scan, which was sent abroad for a specialist to evaluate the images. In his referral papers, Anton is described like this: 'High level show jumper. This horse had bilateral neurectomy BF October 2012'. Such annotations illustrate just how routine Anton's story is in horse sport. The results of the MRI scan were discouraging. Jumping and landing on his injured foot had not done Anton any good, and his owner eventually decided to have him killed. I sent all my documentation to the FEI, and was told the matter would be looked into, but the FEI never reported back, and as far as I know, nobody has been held accountable for what was done to Anton.

Around the same time Anton's story was first published, another tip ticked in about an FEI horse called Never Say Never. Like Anton, Never had undergone one or more neurectomies to mask the pain of chronic injuries in his right front foot. Never's farrier, who had shod him since he was just a colt, took issue with the rider's decision to continue putting pressure on an elderly and chronically injured horse. When the rider wouldn't listen, the farrier alerted the Danish Equestrian Federation to the fact that the horse was de-nerved. This placed the federation in a conundrum, because according to Danish law, any medical treatment of horses, including surgery, which is intended to mask symptoms of illness for the purpose of making the horse able to be trained for or take part in competition, is illegal. However, the Danish Equestrian Federation rules no longer prohibited the use of de-nerved horses in competitions. The ban had been lifted in order to align the national rules with those of the FEI.

Never's rider did not become the subject of a disciplinary investigation for having competed a horse who had undergone performance-enhancing surgery. Nor did anyone report him to the Danish authorities. Instead, the Danish Equestrian Federation quietly informed the rider that an administrative decision had been made that the horse would not be eligible to compete in the future. In any other sport, an athlete who had got off this easily would be thanking his lucky stars, but Never's rider didn't have any other horses as good as Never. Armed with a lawyer, he complained about the decision of the Danish Equestrian Federation to the federation's own Disciplinary Board, and won.[7]

The case made by Never's rider was that the neurectomy had not been performed to get the horse back into competition. It had been done to save his life, because Never was in so much pain from his chronic injuries that the only way for him to have a tolerable retirement was to de-nerve him. The rider claimed that he did not decide to compete Never until after he saw how sound the horse had become, following the neurectomy. Since—according to himself—there was no premeditation, the rider considered that he was in the clear. To support his claim that Never was fit to compete, several vets from the clinic which performed the surgery had verified with skin prick tests that full sensitivity had returned to the limb. This was a good result for the veterinarians as well, because it meant that their clinic was in no way implicated in the performance of illegal, performance-enhancing surgery.

Earlier, I described the hypothetical scenario catered for by the FEI's deregulation of neurectomy. A horse has a debilitating, chronic injury; that horse is de-nerved to put them out of their misery without the need for euthanasia. Then the horse inexplicably recovers, the nerves regenerate

7 Dansk Ride Forbunds Disciplinærudvalg [Danish Equestrian Federation Disciplinary Board], *Kendelse i sag om udelukkelse af hest fra fremtidig deltagelse i konkurrencer* [Decision regarding exclusion of horse from future competition], PDF downloaded from Danish Equestrian Federation website on 17 Jun 2017.

completely, and the horse re-emerges from retirement performing as well as ever. Never's rider claimed that this was what had happened with his horse. And the Danish Equestrian Federation's Disciplinary Board agreed. It agreed, based on a method of assessment which can't work under the best of circumstances, performed by veterinarians from a clinic employed by Never's owner. Such an evaluation is about as credible as WADA asking Dr Fuentes to screen urine samples from his own patients, using a crystal ball.

Soon after, the Danish Equestrian Federation allowed Never to jump at FEI events abroad. At the time, the FEI was not told about Never's de-nerving. Nor did the teams responsible for detecting abnormal limb sensitivity at FEI events pick it up. How could they have, given that the FEI was yet to come up with a method for making such discoveries?

Initially, the Danish Equestrian Federation insisted that everything had gone by the book and that Never was eligible to compete on the Danish team in the Nations Cup in June 2017. As public outcries of disgust began to sound, the federation changed its mind and announced that Never would not be jumping after all. An outright ban on Danish riders competing on de-nerved horses was also re-introduced into the Danish Equestrian Federation rules. But still, nobody was held accountable for allowing a horse to compete at national and international events after undergoing performance-enhancing surgery.

As with Anton, the FEI was sent copies of my information about Never Say Never. As with Anton, the matter would be looked into. The FEI stated in an email that the Danish Equestrian Federation had been asked to provide information regarding the national disciplinary hearing. At the same time, it was confirmed that the deregulation of neurectomy had not been accidental:

> The FEI does not specifically regulate for neurectomy. This is a surgical method which is not classified by the FEI as a banned or a controlled

> method, but if we receive credible evidence that a horse has had a neurectomy or other de-nerving technique, we will investigate as the FEI Veterinary Regulations prevent hyposensitised horses from competing.[8]

So, neurectomy is no longer a banned surgical method; but even though it is not, the FEI will investigate, if presented with credible evidence that a horse has had the operation; because horses with altered limb sensitivity are ineligible to compete, subject to the caveat that the FEI has no way of objectively assessing whether that is the case.

In February 2018, I asked the FEI again for an update on Never's investigation. The question was ignored. However, according to the FEI's database, Never Say Never was back in FEI competition by March that year. Only now, he was competing with a different rider. He jumped three classes without much success. In the first one, he came 19th and won 20 euro. In the second one, he came 60th out of 81 and didn't win any money. The third class saw him place as number 25. Still no money. Next, Never is listed in the FEI database as having been retired from a 150 cm class on 6 April. There are no more results for him after that.

Implications of allowing de-nerved horses in competition

Despite my efforts, it has been impossible to obtain an answer from the FEI as to why the decision was made to remove the ban on riding de-nerved horses in international competition. Let me, then, propose my own explanation.

Modern equestrian sport breaks down the bodies of horses. This can be said with confidence, because numerous studies have documented that there is a connection between the type of discipline for which a horse is used and the type of injury that horse is likely to suffer. For instance, horses who have to land from big jumps and make fast, sharp turns are

8 Email from FEI Communications Department to author, 23 Jun 2017.

more likely to injure their front legs; similarly to the way Anton and Never injured theirs and similarly to how Jet Set, the Swiss Olympic horse who died in Tokyo, injured his. Horses who are used for disciplines that load the hind legs more are at risk of hind leg injuries. There is nothing mysterious or surprising about this well publicised and widely accepted fact.[9]

Whereas racehorses suffer public and catastrophic breakdowns on the track and sometimes have to be shot in front of everyone, the damage done by the Olympic equestrian disciplines is usually more insidious. All the same, it is there. Back pain, tendon and ligament breakdown, arthritis, torn lips, bruised gums, bone damage. One British study revealed that almost half of the participating sport horses, all of whom were presumed sound by their owners, were lame.[10]

The FEI's deregulation of neurectomy surgery solves a problem for the many, many riders who have invested time and money in training a horse who has then become injured and unable to compete. Whereas previously, the rider would have had to engage the services of a specialist doping vet in order to keep competing on their chronically injured horse, now their horse can undergo invisible surgery, which eliminates the need for using drugs to mask that horse's pain. This is now so normalised that there are published, peer-reviewed, scientific studies documenting the efficacy of the intervention.[11]

---

9 R.C. Murray, S. J. Dyson, C. Tranquille and V. Adams, 'Association of type of sport and performance level with anatomical site of orthopaedic injury diagnosis', *Equine Exercise Physiology* 7, Equine vet. J., suppl. 36 (2006), https://beva.onlinelibrary.wiley.com/doi/pdfdirect/10.1111/j.2042-3306.2006.tb05578.x, accessed 21 Aug 2021.

10 Caroline Bankes, 'Half of all sport horses are lame, study finds', *Horse & Hound*, 28 April 2014, https://www.horseandhound.co.uk/news/half-horses-lame-saddle-slip-survey-428728, accessed 21 Aug 2021.

11 Santiago Gutierrez-Nibeyro, N.M. Werpy, Nathaniel White, M.A .Mitchell, R.B. Edwards, R.D. Mitchell, S. Gold, and A.K. Allen, 'Outcome of palmar/plantar digital neurectomy in horses with foot pain evaluated with magnetic resonance imaging: 50 cases (2005-2011)', *Equine Veterinary Journal* 47/2 (2014), https:/www.researchgate.net/publication/260678528_Outcome_of_

Given that the FEI removed its ban on riding de-nerved horses almost a decade ago, and given that riders can now demonstrably compete horses like Anton and Never with impunity, it is impossible to rule out that the London, Rio, and Tokyo Olympics saw chronically injured horses competing after having this performance-enhancing surgery. It is difficult to imagine that the FEI didn't know what it was doing in allowing this to happen.

Aside from the obvious risk to horses from this de-regulation, human safety and integrity is also compromised. Horses have been de-nerved and sold without the knowledge of the buyer. This can be stated with certainty because sometimes, these cases go to court. A rider with the best intentions of clean sportsmanship can unknowingly end up being guilty of competing on a horse with altered limb sensitivity. And a horse with pre-existing, chronic injuries may be at risk of catastrophic breakdown, which also places the rider in harm's way. The IOC wants to protect clean athletes. That aim is not compatible with the FEI's policy on neurectomy.

When I first became aware of all this in 2017, I thought the FEI might have overlooked these consequences of de-regulating performance-enhancing surgery on horses. However, I now know that it must have happened with deliberation, because the FEI has had four years to change the rules back and has opted not to do so. Now you know. When a horse breaks down at or after future Olympic Games and it turns out the horse was competing with a chronic injury, but couldn't feel their pain, you cannot say nobody told you this goes on.

---

palmarplantar_digital_neurectomy_in_horses_with_foot_pain_evaluated_with_magnetic_resonance_imaging_50_cases_2005-2011, accessed 5 Sep 2021. doi: 10.1111/evj.12262

6

Equestrian rules are unenforceable

A fundamental principle of Olympism is the spirit of fair play. But fair play is only possible where clear, enforceable rules exist. In this regard, the FEI has once again shown itself to be unworthy of the Olympic Movement.

IF YOU HAVE EVER WATCHED dressage on TV or in person and wondered what it was for, don't feel bad. Not even the judges know what it's about. They are expected to award scores for things which are not happening, so they are likely to be as confused as you are. The FEI Dressage Rules were originally authored in 1921 and applied to the type of cavalry equitation described in chapter 3. This style of riding is all but gone from the world today, and what you see at FEI dressage competitions is something quite different. It has to be, as it attempts to entertain a wide audience with a short attention span and no real interest in or knowledge about the discipline.

Like other subjectively judged events, such as figure skating and gymnastics, dressage had to de-emphasise its compulsory patterns in the 1990s in order to become more appealing to television viewers, as the FEI relied heavily on IOC funding and the legitimacy which comes with being an Olympic sport. As happened in both figure skating and gymnastics, this decision resulted in more explosive, spectacular and broadly entertaining performances. A survey conducted by Repucom for the FEI in 2014 showed that people who say they are interested in dressage are generally not interested in the discipline because it has anything to do with the training of the horse[1]. This fact is awkward, because the word 'dressage' literally means training. So, even within the limited group of people who say they are interested in dressage, less than one quarter of them are actually interested in the details of dressage. Instead, fans state key motivators like 'aesthetics', 'admiration', 'atmosphere', and 'the horse itself'. Imagine trying to market football, if three-quarters of football fans said they weren't really interested in where the ball went or how it got there.

A growing gap between rules and reality in dressage

All sports change with time and this is not a problem in itself. But because equestrian disciplines—dressage especially—rely on their claim to authenticity and historical relevance, it is not so easy for the FEI to change the rules to fit the modern sport. A good example of this is that, according to the FEI Dressage Rules, the horse's head should be: '... as a rule slightly in front of the vertical ...'[2] Think of a horse or look at a photo of a horse from the side, and notice the front of that horse's face, which is usually a straight or almost straight line. This line should be pointing forwards, according to the FEI Dressage Rules. This is not difficult to achieve. Horses hold their heads in front of the vertical while they stand up and sleep. It's the default orientation of an equine skull. What is difficult is to micro-manage a horse's every movement without causing so much discomfort with how you use the reins that the horse recoils from the

1 FEI, 'Dressage Future', Sports Forum Session 3 presentation, p 2, 27-28 Apr 2015, https://inside.fei.org/system/files/DRE%20Future_Session%203.pdf, accessed 21 Aug 2021.

2 FEI Dressage Rules 2021, Chapter 1, p 9, Article 401.5, https://inside.fei.org/sites/default/files/FEI_Dressage_Rules_2021_Clean_Version_0.pdf, accessed 21 Aug 2021.

pressure of the bits to avoid the discomfort. The unforced, open head and neck carriage mandated by the FEI rules used to be considered the hallmark of a well-schooled horse and a skilled rider. Not because the rider had somehow achieved this carriage, which is natural to horses, but because they had managed not to destroy it with ham-fisted schooling practices. That is why this rule exists.

The problem with the rule is that FEI horses today are trained with their noses deliberately pulled in by the reins, so that the head is not—as a rule—in front of the vertical. In fact, the head of an FEI horse during training and in the warm-up ring is almost exclusively behind the vertical. Sometimes drastically so, because this enables the rider to have more control. In the past few decades, this tendency has crept into the competition arena, so that the highest-scoring dressage horses in the world now perform in front of the judges with their heads behind the vertical, in contravention of the FEI Dressage Rules. Several scientific studies have documented this.[3] The horse's head, which should point forwards—or directly downwards at the most—instead points slightly (or a lot) backwards.

Olympic medals are being awarded to riders who are not even complying with the most basic rule of dressage, which applies from the very first novice competition at the pony club. But the FEI can't simply change the wording in its rules to 'The head should remain in a steady position, as a rule slightly behind the vertical' because this would be an admission that the classical principles of the discipline have been abandoned. The old wording is retained, and the judges simply ignore it.

3 Morgan J. J. O. Lashley, Sandra Nauwelaerts, J.C.M. Vernooij, W. Back, and Hilary M. Clayton, 'Comparison of the head and neck position of elite dressage horses during top-level competitions in 1992 versus 2008', *The Veterinary Journal* 202/3, (2014), https://www.sciencedirect.com/science/article/abs/pii/S1090023314003657, accessed 21 Aug 2021. doi: 10.1016/j.tvjl.2014.08.028

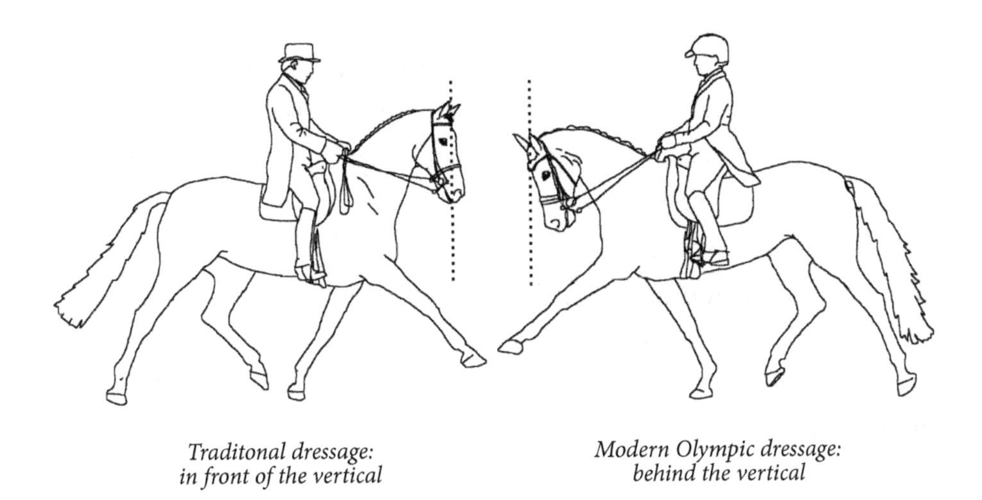

Traditonal dressage: in front of the vertical

Modern Olympic dressage: behind the vertical

In all work, the FEI Dressage Rules also call for '... a supple poll as the highest point of the neck ...'[4] Anatomically, the horse's poll is a bony protrusion at the back of the skull and so not really part of the neck. It's right between the horse's ears, if you want to visualise it. When a Grand Prix horse is moving in accordance with the FEI Dressage Rules, the poll—the area between the ears—will be higher than any part of the horse's neck. This was considered a cardinal rule of cavalry riding, because it was thought to demonstrate an unforced posture, but this too is no longer enforced in modern FEI dressage. I can't find any scientific studies to support this observation, but if you have half an hour, go to YouTube and watch the medal-winning freestyle tests from Rio 2016 or London 2012. If you have access to footage from Tokyo 2020, that works too. If necessary, use the pause button to help you see. You will find that the poll—the spot between the horse's ears—is almost never higher than the highest part of the horse's neck. Again, this is a basic rule which, in theory, applies at all levels of dressage, and which is ignored by judges at Olympic level.

Some people in the sport are going to say that it doesn't matter that much or that it is impossible for a horse with a fat neck to perform with

4 FEI Dressage Rules 2021, Ch 1, p 9, Article 401.5.

the poll as the highest point. There is a heated and ongoing debate about this in equestrian circles. For the IOC, it doesn't matter who is right. The point is that the rule is the rule and it is not enforced. How can this be in the spirit of fair play as demanded by the Olympic Charter?

According to Article 404 in The FEI Dressage Rules, the trot is a 'two-beat pace of alternate diagonal legs',[5] but this definition is also from the days of cavalry riding. Equine biomechanics researchers discovered decades ago that the horses thought by modern judges to have the most impressive gaits were really trotting in four beats. A century ago, this would have been called an 'auctioneer's trot' because, while it takes its toll on the horse's soundness, it 'dazzles the eye of the layman.'[6]

You don't need to have an opinion as to whether the two-beat or the four-beat trot is better. You might think the judges are right and the rules are wrong. Or you might think the rules are right and the judges are wrong. This is also a hotly debated topic in the dressage community, and the IOC does not have to take sides. All you need to do, for the purposes of this chapter, is understand that the two-beat trot, as described in the FEI Dressage Rules, is not currently—and has not been for decades—what wins the medals. This is well established by published, peer-reviewed science, and makes it difficult to introduce measures such as explanatory graphics for television audiences. What would the graphics show? Definitely not any of what is prescribed by the rules of the discipline.

The FEI is in a predicament, because the purity of the gaits and the unforced posture of the horse are considered the cornerstones of dressage.

---

5 FEI Dressage Rules 2021, Ch 1, p 11, Article 404.1, https://inside.fei.org/sites/default/files/FEI_Dressage_Rules_2021_Clean_Version_0.pdf, accessed 21 Aug 2021.

6 Ludwig Koch, *Die Reitkunst im Bilde* [Equestrian Art in Pictures], (Hildesheim, 1998) [first published 1928], 39, https://books.google.dk/books?id=t698Mn_GX7AC&printsec=frontcover&hl=da&source=gbs_ge_summary_r&cad=0#v=onepage&q&f=false, accessed 21 Aug 2021.

Yet, modern science and YouTube have revealed that this is now all make-believe. Unlike other disciplines, the more transparent this one becomes, the less it will make sense to people, because it can't be scored according to its rules.

Add to this that a lot of dressage judging criteria were vague in the first place. For instance, according to the FEI Dressage Rules (2020 version), judges are supposed to evaluate whether the horse in front of them is a 'happy athlete'.[7] Even the most senior scholars in the field of equine cognition and emotions are still debating what it means for a horse to be 'happy'. Dressage judges possess no credentials to make them authorities on this. The FEI has been aware of the problem since the concept of the 'happy athlete' was introduced in 2004. Industry specialist, Dr Eric van Breda, broke the news at the Global Dressage Forum that year, according to the FEI's own summary of the event: 'Dr Eric van Breda emphasised that "happiness" cannot be measured in equine athletes in the same way as in human athletes. A horse has no concept of training for a goal, and does not fill out questionnaires.'[8] Nevertheless, it sounds nice with happy horse athletes, even if horses aren't athletes and judges can't tell if they are happy, so the FEI has kept the requirement in every subsequent revision of its rules.

Implications for fairness in judging

The rhythm of the gaits, the harmony between horse and rider, and the balance and impulsion described in the rules are all either absent or indefinable. This leaves dressage judges presiding over nothing more than a beauty pageant. As a result, the world of dressage is mired in a

7 FEI Dressage Rules 2021, Ch 1, p 9, Article 401.1.

8 FEI, 'The Horse as a "Happy Athlete"', 4 Dec 2004, https://inside.fei.org/media-updates/2004-global-dressage-forum, accessed 21 Aug 2021.

permanent judging crisis. Unlike judges in other subjectively scored disciplines, dressage judges are statistically more likely to disagree on the highest-scoring performances than on mediocre ones. This means that top placings are often controversial. It means that the wrong people have been given Olympic medals and that this will continue to happen. When judges must award scores for criteria that either don't exist or are in no way met, it seems unlikely that they can avoid being influenced by the reputation of the rider in front of them. Just before the Tokyo Olympic Games kicked off, British Olympic medallist Laura Tomlinson had this to say in an opinion piece for *Horse & Hound*:

> With electronic scoring making marks more transparent, it looked as though the marking would improve. However, it seems that when a top name has a 'boo-boo', they may go down to marks of four for that movement – but will be compensated heavily for this with everything good thereafter, so that the end score is often still unrealistic.[9]

Does this provide athletes with a level playing field in the spirit of fair play? No, it doesn't. It never will.

Researchers Hugues Mercier and Sandro Heiniger looked into the judging in eight Olympic disciplines. Even among other subjectively judged disciplines, dressage stood out as having 'a significant amount of subjectivity in the judging process compared to other sports with similar judging systems.' The explanation for this, according to the researchers, may be that some criteria of excellence in dressage, such as elegance and beauty, may be too difficult to agree upon.

9 Laura Tomlinson, 'Olympic judges, please mark what you see, not who you see', *Horse & Hound*, 20 July 2021, https://www.horseandhound.co.uk/plus/opinion/laura-tomlinson-olympic-judges-marking-753444, accessed 21 Aug 2021.

> The simplest explanation is that judges fundamentally disagree on what constitutes an above average dressage performance. This might be due to imprecise or overly subjective judging guidelines, or to the difficulty or unwillingness of judges to apply said guidelines objectively. No matter the reason, our analysis reveals a clear and systemic judging problem in dressage, and we recommend that the FEI thoroughly reviews its judging practices.[10]

The FEI is—as always—in the process of doing just that, but dressage will still face the same unsolvable dilemma. Modern Olympic dressage horses cannot move in accordance with the most basic definitions of correct posture and purity of gaits set forth in the FEI Dressage Rules. Even if they could, nobody would want to watch them on TV. It would be like watching figure skating from the 1960s. A handful of purists would be tickled pink, but the world in general would still change the channel.

A welfare code incompatible with the reality of horse sport

In jumping and eventing, the judging can be more objective, because obstacles are either cleared within the time allowed or they are not. But that doesn't mean that all the rules of these disciplines are enforced. Like the rules for other disciplines, the FEI rules for jumping and eventing begin with the FEI Code of Conduct for the Welfare of the Horse, which states that 'Welfare of the horse must never be subordinated to competitive or commercial influences'.[11]

10 Sandro Heiniger and Hugues Mercier, 'Judging the Judges: A General Framework for Evaluating the Performance of International Sports Judges', https://arxiv.org/pdf/1807.10055.pdf, accessed 21 Aug 2021.

11 FEI Jumping Rules, 25th edition, Code of Conduct For the Welfare of the Horse, 2021, 8, https://inside.fei.org/sites/default/files/Jumping_Rules_2021_clean.pdf, accessed 21 Aug 2021; and FEI, Eventing Rules, 25th edition, Code of Conduct For the Welfare of the Horse, 2021, 10, https://inside.fei.org/sites/default/files/Eventing%20Rules%20for%202021%20-%20clean%20version%20-%2010.12.2020_0.pdf, accessed 21 Aug 2021.

The trouble with the Code of Conduct is that 'welfare' is at least as flimsy a concept as 'beauty', 'harmony' or 'happiness'. Horse welfare can mean any number of things, depending on whom you ask. When Dr Iris Bergmann from the University of Sydney looked into welfare concepts in horse racing, she found that the same images of thoroughbred horses were interpreted differently by industry insiders than they were by representatives from animal advocacy groups.[12] This should not surprise anyone. What passes for 'horse welfare' in equestrian circles is highly variable and can include some training and management practices which are directly harmful for horses, such as permanent stabling or the use of painful equipment. This makes the rules impossible to enforce.

There is an evidence-based model of animal welfare called 'The Five Domains'. It was originally developed by animal welfare scientist Professor David J Mellor from Massey University in New Zealand. In its 25 years of existence, The Five Domains model has become widely accepted and is regularly updated to include new evidence. Dr Roly Owers sings its praises when he speaks at FEI meetings, even though—taken at face value—The Five Domains model renders equestrian sport impracticable.

In 2020, The Five Domains model was updated by Professor Mellor and a team of his colleagues to explicitly describe negative and positive impacts of human behaviour in our interactions with animals. Some common practices of elite equestrians are flagged as having severe negative impacts on horse welfare. This includes the use of restrictive equipment such as bits and nosebands which can prevent horses from expressing natural behaviours. Several husbandry practices commonly considered necessary and beneficial in the equestrian industry also come under fire for the effect they have on the mental state of horses, such as 'the yearning

12 Iris Bergmann, 'Naturalness and the Legitimacy of Thoroughbred Racing: A Photo-Elicitation Study with Industry and Animal Advocacy Informants', *Animals* 10/9 (2020), https://www.researchgate.net/publication/343926314_Naturalness_and_the_Legitimacy_of_Thoroughbred_Racing_A_Photo-Elicitation_Study_with_Industry_and_Animal_Advocacy_Informants, accessed 7 Sep 2021. doi: 10.3390/ani10091513

for company (i.e., loneliness) of isolated individuals of social species kept in separate enclosures' and 'the daily thwarting of normal long-duration grazing motivation in stabled horses fed with highly concentrated feeds which nevertheless meet their nutritional requirements.'[13]

Locking horses up, feeding them a species-inappropriate diet, rendering them socially bereft, and preventing them from expressing their natural behaviour are all considered necessary interventions by those involved in FEI sport. In an equestrian context, 'horse welfare' therefore means whatever you want it to mean. People make up their own definitions to suit themselves and therefore the word ends up rather meaningless. However, given that travel exposes horses to illness and stress, equestrian sport breaks horses' bodies, and the life of an elite competition horse usually involves living alone in a cage, it will be glaringly obvious by now to anyone outside the FEI family that horse sport is basically all about subordinating the welfare of the horse to competitive and commercial influences. By default, almost every athlete is in violation of the Code of Conduct for the Welfare of the Horse and therefore also of FEI rules.

The Code of Conduct stipulates that 'Stabling and feeding must be compatible with the best Horse management practices.' It does not explain what is meant by 'best', and so this rule is meaningless. The Code of Conduct states that 'Horses must only undergo training that matches their physical capabilities and level of maturity for their respective disciplines.' If this were enforced, we would not see discipline-specific injuries or hear a six times Olympic vet casually mention that a lot of horses are on illegal, undetectable pain killers. The Code of Conduct demands that 'Tack [i.e. the bridle, saddle etc] must be designed and fitted to avoid the risk of pain or injury'. Yet, several scientific studies

13 David J. Mellor, Ngaio J Beausoleil, Katharine E Littlewood, Andrew N McLean, Paul D. McGreevy, Bidda Jones and Christina Wilkins, 'The 2020 Five Domains Model: Including Human-Animal Interactions in Assessment of Animal Welfare', *Animals*, 10/10 (2020), https://doi.org/10:3390/ani10101870

have shown that most horses at FEI competitions are made to endure restrictive nosebands, and riders are practically never held accountable.[14]

In 2019, the International Society for Equitation Science (ISES) issued a position statement calling out the FEI for not protecting horses against pain and injury from nosebands:

> The scarcity of reported incidents of riders being penalised for excessively tightened nosebands in competition suggests a lack of objective monitoring of noseband-related guidelines and recommendations. Subjective noseband tightness checks performed without a uniform approach including use of a standardised tool at the frontal nasal plane will result in inconsistent measurements and outcomes. Horse welfare may be compromised as a result.[15]

The noseband issue is an embarrassing problem for the FEI, because it cannot simply tell its show stewards to enforce noseband rules. This would allow horses to open their mouths to reduce the pain from the bit or bits. In some cases, riders would lose control. In others, the public would merely be put off by the sight of a gaping mouth and a blue, hypoxic tongue. An unmuzzled horse tends to scatter the equestrian fantasy of beauty, harmony, and intuitive understanding.

In 2020, a scientific collaboration between researchers in Australia and Mexico provided the first radiographic evidence that sport horses develop bone lesions at the site of the noseband. In the study, 37.5 percent of 144 participating horses (used for dressage, jumping, and eventing as well as military parades) were found to have nasal bone lesions and

---

14 Orla Doherty, Vincent Casey, Paul McGreevy, and Sean Arkins, 'Noseband Use in Equestrian Sports - An International Study'. *PLoS One*, 12/1 (2017) e0169060, https://pubmed.ncbi.nlm.nih.gov/28045961/. doi:10.1371/journal.pone.0169060

15 International Society for Equitation Science, 'Position statement on restrictive nosebands', 2019, https://equitationscience.com/equitation/position-statement-on-restrictive-nosebands, accessed 21 Aug 2021.

13.8 percent had radiographic changes to the mandible. The authors take pains to highlight that no causal link has been established, but also express concern regarding the ubiquitous use of tight, restrictive nosebands in equestrian sport.[16]

Enforcement of the Code of Conduct may be impossible for the FEI, but the purpose of the code was never to be followed. It is a public relations tool devised at a time when camera phones and social media didn't exist, and the FEI was mostly in control of what images and information regarding horse sport were available to the public.

The Code of Conduct for the Welfare of the Horse was first conceived in 1990, after one of the FEI's biggest stars, a two-times Olympic medallist, was caught on camera using a training technique which is classed by the FEI as a form of horse abuse, and the scandal blew up in international media. Since then, the standard FEI response, when its use of horses is questioned, has been to repeat the mantra from the Code of Conduct: 'The welfare of the horse is paramount at all times.'

Inventing such an unenforceable code moved horse sport management out of the frying pan and into the fire. Instead of just having some problems with cheating and horse abuse, the FEI had now saddled its athletes with a Code of Conduct that contradicted the very essence of horse sport.

The stewards at international horse shows cannot enforce the Code of Conduct, because doing so amounts to accusing an international star athlete to their face of mistreating an animal, which makes for a very unpleasant situation for the stewards. Since rollkur (an explanation of this will follow in the next chapter) was first banned by the FEI in 2008 as a form of abuse, this ubiquitous technique has continued to be

16 Lucia Pérez-Manrique, Karina León-Pérez, Emmanuel Zamora-Sánchez, Sarah Davies, Christopher Ober, Bethany Wilson, and Paul McGreevy, 'Prevalence and Distribution of Lesions in the Nasal Bones and Mandibles of a Sample of 144 Riding Horses', *Animals* 10/9 (2020), 1661. https://doi.org/10.3390/ani10091661.

applied with impunity by riders—including at the Olympic Games. To my knowledge, no rider has ever been sanctioned for this offence, which is openly practised at FEI events, right in front of the stewards. Photo bans and harassment are used to prevent independent journalists and concerned spectators from documenting what is going on.

In this regard, the FEI faces yet another unsolvable sports governance problem of its own making. If horses are supposed to be happy athletes and if their welfare is supposed to be paramount, then any photo of a horse in distress at an FEI event is evidence that the rider is in violation of the Code of Conduct. Horse shows are full of horses who don't want to be there, who try to escape, and who are punished for it by their riders. Thanks to Saint Boy, the flogged modern pentathlon horse from the Tokyo Olympic Games, the public is now better aware of this than ever before. It was fairly easy to keep it a secret in 1990, but today, that is impossible. We could all see horses having a miserable time in Tokyo. Saint Boy was not the only one. Jet Set had a catastrophic breakdown on the cross-country course, which cost him his life. Irish horse Alejandro suffered what would be best described as a panic attack and landed on several jumps before finally taking a dangerous nosedive. Both horse and rider were able to limp out, but the new jumping format had done nothing to ensure the safety of either. Everyone watching at home could see that. In the old format, Alejandro's rider, Shane Sweetnam, would have retired as soon as he could feel things going wrong. In the new format with three riders per team and no drop-score, such a decision would have meant the end of Ireland's Olympic team jumping. Sweetnam was placed in the unenviable position of having to choose between the safety and welfare of himself and his horse and trying his best to reach the Olympic goals of his team. This is guaranteed to keep happening with the 'smaller teams, more flags' approach.

There was a time when photos of horses falling on the cross-country course, being whipped, or visibly resisting their riders during a dressage test were printed in equestrian magazines and books. It did not use to be forbidden to talk about horses not wanting to jump or being bothered by the rider's actions. It was just a fact of the sport that humans competed on horses for their own sakes and not in order to enrich those horses' lives. The advent of the FEI Code of Conduct and, subsequently, the social construct of the horse as a 'happy equine athlete' and 'team-mate' may have bought the sport a little time in a world increasingly conscious of animal exploitation. But it also created a necessity for the FEI to sweep everything under the carpet that wasn't all sunshine and lollipops for the horses. Doing this requires a gigantic carpet, because there isn't much about modern horse sport that does not bother the horses. It made enforcement of the rules impossible and public relations a nightmare. The advent of the internet would soon make it all much, much worse.

7

The impact of social media

With the advent of YouTube videos and camera phones, the gap between official claims and what actually happens to horses at equestrian events is becoming obvious to audiences worldwide. This is leading to increasing calls for Equestrian to be dropped from the Olympics.

'CHANGE OR BE CHANGED' IS the motto of Olympic Agenda 2020. The FEI has for decades refused to move with the times regarding horse welfare, and now its public image is fast going down the drain. The emergence of camera phones and social media means the FEI no longer controls its public image with an iron fist as it used to do. It has become impossible to hide what happens to horses at its competitions. The question you should be asking yourself is whether the IOC can afford to be associated with such a federation.

The story of rollkur is ideal for illustrating how Equestrian has become the Jonah of the Olympic family. The story is a bit long because it spans several decades, but it is also funny at times (unless you are a horse) in all its absurdity.

The FEI can publish as many conference agendas and meeting summaries and tribunal decisions and live-streamed presentations of internal regulation revisions on its website as it wants. It cannot lay claim to being a transparent federation.

In 1992, one of the most controversial phenomena in the history of equestrian sport was given a name: Rollkur. The term is German and literally means 'rolling cure'. It refers to an old remedy for digestive problems, which had to be swallowed, whereupon the patient had to roll around to coat the inside of their stomach. Rollkur, in an equestrian context, is a pun which plays on the fact that some riders attempt to fix—or cure—problems in the basic schooling of their horses by rolling up the horse's neck, thereby disarming a horse who would otherwise resist them. Horses need their necks for leverage when they want to access their full strength. If you take away a horse's control of their neck, they become far easier to subjugate.

A well-trained cavalry horse could be ridden by almost anyone. That was the purpose of the campaign school. A Grand Prix horse schooled in the old way was even easier to ride. There was a time when beginners were always put on advanced horses, because these were considered the safest and easiest to ride. The spectacular performances increasingly expected of modern sport horses, and the abandonment of the basic rules of schooling which had once rendered horses safe and fit for purpose, meant that by the end of the 1980s, getting in the saddle of a Grand Prix horse was becoming an extreme sport. Some dressage riders now relied on coercive riding techniques to contain the explosive power necessary to produce the frenzied goose-stepping favoured by the judges and the crowds.

The emergence of 'rollkur'

Through backwards traction on the reins—sometimes aided by gadgets based on pulleys or levers—riders put their horses in a posture where the horse's nose almost touched their chest. This happened at home and in the warm-up arena at both dressage and jumping competitions. Riders could be seen leaning back in the saddle, pushing their feet forward into the stirrups, and seemingly putting all the weight they could muster into the reins connected to the metal bits in the horse's mouth. Sometimes even a side-to-side 'seesawing' action of the hands, once condemned at even the humblest riding establishment as a sign of incompetence, began to emerge among elite international riders.

The staff at the German horse magazine, *St Georg*, came up with the term rollkur. It first accompanied a notice about the practice in 1992, but it was not until 2005 that the controversy was to really kick off. *St Georg* published a scathing article featuring photos of named dressage riders, claiming that these riders were compromising the welfare of their horses by forcing them into extreme postures.[1]

This caused fierce debate in the international dressage community. Were the photos real? Had they been altered? Were they representative of how the riding took place? If they were, could it really be that riders were intentionally harming their horses? It was not customary for dressage fans to question the opinions of the judges or the riding of the stars, but now that began to happen in some quarters. In the photos published, the horses appeared to be put under pressure by this type of riding. On the other hand, it was unthinkable to many fans that the world's most successful riders should be anything but kind and conscientious in how they schooled their horses.

'Anything forced or misunderstood can never be beautiful', goes one equestrian platitude. The quote is attributed to the Greek author Xenophon (c. 430–350 BCE), who—nevertheless—advocated for horses to be whipped and starved as part of their training. Most horsey people have not actually read Xenophon, but the quote is very popular, and its message widely accepted. If only unforced things can be beautiful, then it follows that nothing which is beautiful can ever be forced. It is soothing

1 *St. Georg* staff, 'Dressur Pervers' [Perverted Dressage], *St. Georg*, Jul 2005, https://www.st-georg.de/hintergrund/rollkur/dressur-pervers-aus-st-georg-juli2005/, accessed 21 Aug 2021.

to think that whatever happens to please the senses can automatically be assumed to be morally right. When their favourite rider is accused of cruelty, a fan is forced to consider the possibility that they have been ignorant in their appreciation of that rider. Alternatively, Xenophon may have been mistaken, and something forced can be beautiful after all, which—for the average equestrian fan—opens up a large and unwelcome can of worms.

One rider featured in the *St Georg* article, Anky van Grunsven, who had won her sixth Olympic medal the year before in Athens, sued the magazine and won. Mrs Van Grunsven's coach and husband, Sjeff Janssen, also made legal threats to other media outlets who had helped spread photos and footage of their training. Mr Janssen said that the way his pupils trained was for the physical welfare of the horse. The technique, which he preferred to call 'Low, Deep and Round' or 'LDR', was an advanced tool for suppling and strengthening elite horses. It was only for expert riders, and the position was never induced with force or for more than ten or twenty seconds at a time.[2]

For 13 years after *St Georg* first wrote about rollkur, the smouldering dissent had been ignored and allowed to fester by the FEI. All this time, the riders alleged to be using it had been winning, and the practice had become widespread. Rollkur was practised by several of the new megastars, who had been breathing life into dressage since the advent of the musical freestyle. Now, with the 2005 article and the court case, there was a public scandal.

The newly established Welfare Subcommittee of the FEI Veterinary Department was given the job of coordinating investigations into rollkur. It was announced that there would be a workshop at the Olympic Museum

2 Astrid Appels, 'Sjef Janssen, Dr. Rene van Weeren and Anky van Grunsven on Coaching and Hyperflexion', Eurodressage, 6 Nov 2006, https://www.eurodressage.com/2006/11/06/sjef-janssen-dr-rene-van-weeren-and-anky-van-grunsven-coaching-and-hyperflexion, accessed 3 Oct 2021.

in Lausanne on 31 January in 2006, where stakeholders and experts would meet to discuss the problem. Represented in Lausanne were riders, coaches, veterinarians, officials and scientists. They decided to get rid of the name rollkur, because it was felt that the moniker coined by *St Georg* carried connotations of abuse. From now on, rollkur would refer only to the prolonged and excessive bending of a horse's neck, which all agreed was unacceptable, whereas the brief and gentle technique supposedly applied by skilled professionals for seconds at a time would be termed 'hyperflexion of the neck.'

There was disagreement at the workshop as to whether hyperflexion of the neck had a place in equestrian sport under any circumstances. The evidence that it was beneficial for the horse was extremely sketchy. It has since been conceded by the only scientist who is on the record as defending the technique as a gymnastic exercise in Lausanne that the main purpose of hyperflexion is the subjugation of reactive horses. However, there was also no conclusive evidence that the technique caused long-term damage. Everyone at the workshop agreed that hyperflexion should only be performed for very short periods of time and that it should never be forced on the horse.[3]

A press release was subsequently issued, stating that there was no scientific evidence that hyperflexion caused long-term damage if it was performed by expert riders, and that the horse's welfare was considered paramount by the FEI.[4]

YouTube and the impact of video

This would probably have bought the FEI another 13 years of peace and

3 FEI, 'Report of the FEI Veterinary and Dressage Committees' Workshop: The use of over bending ("Rollkur") in FEI Competition', 31 Jan 2006 (Updated and revised version published 5 Mar 2006), no longer available online.

4 FEI 'Workshop in Lausanne', media update, 31 Jan 2006, https://inside.fei.org/media-updates/fei-workshop-lausanne, accessed 21 Aug 2021.

quiet, had YouTube not been launched the year before. In Holland, an Austrian veterinarian and activist called Dr Ulrike Thiel began that year to film riders during their warm-up routines and was posting the videos online as documentation of hyperflexion in practice. In Sweden, an illustrator and dressage rider called Theresa Sandin used her website as a platform to campaign against the technique. Whilst hyperflexion of the neck was clearly being applied by experts—including some Olympians—it did not otherwise appear to be applied as advertised.

In March 2008, my colleague, Luise Thomsen, and I were at the Danish Warmblood Stallion Licensing show in Herning, where a press conference with Anky van Grunsven was taking place. Having seen Dr Thiel's footage on YouTube and read Ms Sandin's website, we wanted to find out if Mrs van Grunsven would re-commit to previous statements by her husband and trainer about the brevity of hyperflexion spells.

We had one question: 'What is the maximum length of time you would ever ask a horse to stay in the hyperflexed position?' Mrs van Grunsven didn't immediately answer the question, and it was necessary to ask several times. In the end, Mrs van Grunsven admitted that she didn't know. 'I don't have a clue,' she said. 'Time flies when you're having fun.' Mrs van Grunsven confirmed that several minutes at a time was not out of the question.

The Olympic rider and multiple gold medallist also stated that she would never force a horse into the hyperflexed position with her reins. 'It would always be not pulling. It would never be a fight,' she said. This appeared—from our footage of Mrs van Grunsven's riding in the warm-up arena at the same event—to be debatable.

We slowed down a sequence from the warm-up arena where Mrs van Grunsven's horse appeared to attempt to wrestle free of the hyperflexed position, whereupon his rider put him back there. The use of slow motion was intended to illustrate to viewers what not pulling and never fighting looked like according to Anky van Grunsven. These words mean different things to different people, so they are useless until you know what is meant by the person who is saying them. Some people thought the slowed video of Mrs van Grunsven never pulling or fighting looked fine. Others thought it looked like pulling and fighting. The video is on YouTube if you want to see it and decide for yourself. It's called 'Anky van Grunsven talks about her method'.[5]

For the purposes of the IOC evaluating the appropriateness of dressage in the Olympics, it doesn't matter in this context whether you agree with hyperflexion of the neck or not. What matters is that FEI riders and show organisers now find themselves in need of keeping it a secret, which is becoming more and more difficult.

Hyperflexion of the neck has been a nightmare for the FEI for the past 15 years, because it speaks for itself. The claim that riders only hyperflexed their horses for a few seconds as a suppling exercise relied on only photographic evidence being available to the public. YouTube changed all that, and the FEI had not foreseen the problems it would cause.

Having initially reassured fans that hyperflexion was harmless in the hands of skilled professionals, the FEI Veterinary Committee suddenly declared in April 2008 that the technique was now considered by the FEI to be a form of mental abuse. Almost as an afterthought, this monumental admission—that for years and years, medals were given to riders who had, according to the FEI, been abusing their horses—was made via a press release about a meeting of the Veterinary Committee. No other announcements were made on the topic by the FEI. The brief statement read as follows:

> There are no known clinical side effects specifically arising from the use of hyperflexion, however there are serious concerns for a horse's well-being if the technique is not practiced correctly. The FEI condemns

5 Epona TV, 'Anky van Grunsven Talks About her Method', YouTube video, 26 Oct 2009, https://www.youtube.com/watch?v=svOBsSdjUvU.

> hyperflexion in any equestrian sport as an example of mental abuse. The FEI states that it does not support the practice.[6]

Since abuse of the horse was against FEI rules, this meant that riders were going to have to make do without hyperflexion at the impending Olympic Games in Beijing (where the equestrian competitions were scheduled to be held in Hong Kong due to biosecurity issues). Then, suddenly, the Veterinary Committee press release was edited to remove the statement that hyperflexion was mental abuse. It was not possible at that time to get an answer from the FEI as to why the press release had been altered or whether the ban on hyperflexion of the neck had been rescinded.

As the 2008 Olympic Games began, photos of the dressage warm-up in Hong Kong showed high-profile riders being allowed by the FEI stewards to hyperflex their horses. How could this be, given that the FEI had announced a few months earlier that this training technique was a form of abuse?

According to Dr. Frits Sluyter, head of the FEI's Veterinary Department at the time, the explanation was that it was 'not practical' to enforce a ban on hyperflexion during the Olympic Games. Anky van Grunsven, who had been photographed riding her horse in the hyperflexed position during a schooling session in Hong Kong, subsequently won her third individual Olympic dressage gold medal in a row.

In 2009, the FEI inexplicably disbanded its welfare subcommittee, which had only held its inaugural meeting in May 2005, and which had originally been given the task of looking into rollkur. It has been impossible to get the FEI to explain why this was done.

The same year, more precisely in October 2009, Luise Thomsen and I needed some footage of gait abnormalities for an educational video on

6 Quoted in Fran Jurga, 'Rollkur Revolt: FEI Makes Official Statement Discouraging Overflexion in Dressage Training', *Equus* magazine, 18 Apr 2008, https://equusmagazine.com/blog-equus/rollkur-revolt-fei-makes-official-statement-discouraging-overflexion-in-dressage-training, accessed 21 Aug 2021.

musculoskeletal problems in the horse. Competition horses are often unsound, and the FEI World Cup qualifier event in Odense would be an ideal place to obtain such footage. The purpose of our trip was not to seek out controversy. We had already had plenty of that in 2009, when our footage from FEI and Danish Equestrian Federation events was used in a sports exposé on Danish television. An internationally renowned scholar in horse behaviour and welfare, Professor Jan Ladewig from the University of Copenhagen, said on national television that, in his opinion, the riders depicted in the footage were violating Danish animal protection law. He also said that in equestrian sport, similar things happen to lots of horses every day.[7] There was much commotion before eventually it all died down as it tends to do.

When we drove to Odense, Luise and I were not planning to kick off another scandal, let alone an international one. We were not even intending to film the Grand Prix riders. We were interested in the horses competing in the young horse championships at the same event. After a long day of filming, we were on our way to the car when we saw a striking chestnut horse being ridden in hyperflexion. This seemed to be going on for more than twenty seconds. Luise whipped out the camera and started filming. We ended up standing there for hours.

There were other riders who were also hyperflexing their horses, but the chestnut transfixed us because he seemed never to get a break. At one point he cantered closely by, and his tongue could be seen hanging out of his mouth. It was blue. The rider seemed to notice, and halted his horse. Without releasing the tension in the reins, he leant forward and stuffed the tongue back into the horse's mouth. Then he continued riding in the same manner.

Veterinarians had told us about horses' tongues going blue from the severe pressure of the bits, which is necessary to induce the hyperflexed posture. However, we had never seen a blue tongue like this, let alone

---

7 Lige På og Sport, TV2, 30 Apr 2009.

had a chance to film it. Mostly, horses keep their tongues inside their mouths. One of the purposes of restrictive nosebands is to hide the horse's squashed and often discoloured tongue from judges, spectators and—especially—photographers. But this horse's limp, blue tongue was in full view. In the footage, several spectators are staring at it, seemingly in disgust. We didn't know who the rider was and we weren't entirely sure what we had on tape until we had arrived home to load the footage. Then we realised.

'Do you understand that this is probably the worst rollkur footage anyone in the world has ever published?' Luise asked. She forgot to call it by its polite name, hyperflexion. I did understand. I had never seen footage like this before either. But what were we going to do with it? So far, we had not been able to get the FEI to have any opinions about the footage we had published. We were too small and local to Denmark.

At the time, we ran a subscription-based streaming service because we wanted to be independent of advertising revenue, so that we could cover both the scientific and the controversial issues we had not been allowed to prioritise when we were previously employed by a glossy horse magazine. All our content was behind a paywall. The subscription model was great for our independence, but we were also a niche within a niche, preaching to a choir of people who already shared our values to the extent that they gave us their money every month.

We decided that the blue tongue footage was going on YouTube, so that enough people could see it that the FEI would be forced to answer our questions. What happened to the ban on hyperflexion? Why did you disband your Welfare Subcommittee? Again, the footage was slowed to make sure it was impossible for viewers to miss that blue tongue. One problem with horse sport is that most spectators—and even judges and stewards—miss the obvious signs of pain and discomfort constantly shown by horses. A recent study by Dr Catherine Bell and her colleagues at the Equine Behaviour and Training Association in the UK showed that 85 percent of equestrians—regardless of experience, and including equestrian industry professionals—failed to recognise signs of negative emotions in horses.[8] (I am honoured to be listed as a co-author of this study, but I am only included because I sourced the video clips used by Dr Bell and others to gather this crucial information.)

Slowed footage and high-quality still images can sometimes help people see what they otherwise miss. Before Luise and I uploaded the original four-and-a-half-minute version of what would become known as 'the blue tongue video', we had to find out who the rider was and call him to offer him a right of reply. His name was Patrik Kittel and he was an Olympic rider from Sweden.

I called Mr Kittel to tell him that we had filmed him schooling his horse, Scandic, at the FEI World Cup show in Odense. I informed him I was taping the call. I asked him if he thought he had been riding in accordance with the FEI Code of Conduct. Mr Kittel said he would like the question in an email with the footage so he could show it to his lawyers. When I asked him if he didn't know whether he had been riding in accordance with the Code of Conduct, he replied: 'Of course I do. Otherwise the steward would have done something.' We complied with his request to send the footage and questions by email, but Mr Kittel never replied.

Luise spoke on the phone with the FEI Chief Steward who had been responsible for the warm-up in Odense, who said that complaints had been made about Mr Kittel's riding, but because it was deemed no worse than that of other riders at the World Cup show, it was decided not to intervene.

We sent the footage to the FEI with the usual questions and received an automatic reply to let us know that Communications Director Richard

8 Catherine Bell, Suzanne Rogers, Julie Taylor and Debbie Busby, 'Improving the Recognition of Equine Affective States', *Animals,* 9/12 (2019), https://www.researchgate.net/publication/337941121_Improving_the_Recognition_of_Equine_Affective_States, accessed Aug 2021. doi: 10.3390/ani9121124

Johnson was out of the office but would be checking messages. That was on 18 October. Then nothing. On 20 October 2009, we made the video of Scandic public on YouTube with the title 'Blue Tongue World Cup'.[9] Again, we asked the same simple question we had asked Mr. Kittel and the FEI in vain: 'is this in accordance with the Code of Conduct of the FEI?' Not long after publication, someone tried to have the video taken down from YouTube, claiming that it violated their privacy. YouTube accepted our explanation that the video depicted international athletes at a major sporting event and was relevant to the public debate, and it was not removed.

The YouTube clip spread like wildfire on social media. The website of British Dressage crashed because of the debate it caused, and a ban on discussing the blue tongue video was imposed on users. International horse media immediately picked up the story. Then mainstream media followed. *The Guardian* published a news story called 'Olympics row over horse "cruelty"' which described the tens of thousands of people signing petitions and the threats to boycott dressage at the 2012 Olympics. American fans were planning to protest against rollkur at the Dressage World Championships in Kentucky the following year. The Chairman of the British Horse Society, Patrick Print, wrote an open letter to FEI President Princess Haya, demanding an investigation. Still, we had received no reply from the FEI.

Some people were saying that they didn't believe us and that we had probably patched together snippets of hyperflexion footage of Scandic to make his rider look bad. So on 26 October, we uploaded the maximum length of uncut footage which it was possible to post from a basic YouTube account at the time: ten minutes. It was shaky and not all of Scandic, but it showed that we had by no means exhausted our raw footage when we made the first clip. There was plenty more where that came from.

9 Epona TV, 'Blue Tongue World Cup', YouTube video, 20 Oct 2009, https://www.youtube.com/watch?v=8hIXGiV4N4k.

By 27 October, we had still not heard back from the FEI communications department. Instead, the federation's legal department reached out. They wanted us to surrender our raw footage for the investigation they were now forced by public opinion to instigate against Mr Kittel, even though his riding had gone without comment from the FEI stewards on the day of the competition. We eventually told them they couldn't have any footage apart from what we had already made available on YouTube. If the FEI was unable to govern its own disciplines without the help of the equestrian press, then it had a problem in need of solving. It was this problem we were trying to highlight by publishing the footage in the first place.

Patrik Kittel said in the press that he did not think the incident would have any consequences for him. It appears he was right. The FEI let him hyperflex Scandic again at the Olympic Games in London 2012. Today, Mr Kittel sits on the FEI's Dressage Committee, making policy for the sport.

From 'rollkur' to 'hyperflexion' to 'LDR': plus ça change

It was announced that there would be another workshop on hyperflexion in Lausanne in February 2010. Many of the same people as had been there in 2006 were invited. Presumably, many of the same conversations were had. After the conference, the FEI announced that the problem with hyperflexion had now been successfully resolved. 'FEI Round-Table Resolves Rollkur Controversy', proclaimed the press release.[10] That is something of an overstatement. What was decided at the 2010 rollkur workshop in Lausanne was the same as had been decided at the rollkur workshop in 2006. The top riders would continue to ride as they pleased.

10 FEI, 'FEI Round-Table Conference Resolves Rollkur Controversy', 8 Feb 2010, https://inside.fei.org/media-updates/fei-round-table-conference-resolves-rollkur-controversy, accessed 21 Aug 2021.

The FEI would claim publicly that coercive riding was not allowed. The welfare of the horse would be paramount at all times.

'Following constructive debate at the FEI round-table conference at the IOC Headquarters in Lausanne today (9 February), the consensus of the group was that any head and neck position of the horse achieved through aggressive force is not acceptable,' read the FEI's statement.[11] This was the same as what had been decided in 2006. All delegates at the first workshop agreed that horses should not be forced into the hyperflexed posture. At the meeting in 2010, this was agreed upon again.

'The group redefined hyperflexion/Rollkur as flexion of the horse's neck achieved through aggressive force, which is therefore unacceptable.' In the four years that had passed since 2006, the polite term, 'hyperflexion of the neck', had taken on the same connotations of abuse which had made delegates at the 2006 workshop decide that the name rollkur needed an upgrade. In 2006, the workshop had agreed to distinguish between rollkur and hyperflexion as respectively unacceptable and acceptable techniques. By 2010, it was clear that they were the same thing and therefore equally offensive to spectators, regardless of the terminology used.

Rollkur—by any name—is upsetting for a lot of people to behold and will cause a scandal if filmed and published, which is why many insiders found the next sentence darkly funny at the time: 'The technique known as Long, Deep and Round (LDR), which achieves flexion without undue force, is acceptable.' LDR is the name that riders themselves use to describe what others call rollkur or hyperflexion. Sometimes the L stands for long, and sometimes it stands for low, but the technique is the same. Riders insist that they don't use force. Photographs and video footage raise questions as to the accuracy of such claims.

As if stewards had not had a difficult job enforcing the rules before, they now had to police a technique which was simultaneously banned and allowed. They had to read the mind of each rider who applied LDR

11 FEI, 'FEI Round-Table Conference'.

during their warm-up session to ensure that any force applied was due ('undue force' being frowned upon) and non-aggressive. And not long after the initial press release, the FEI added another criterion. No head and neck position could be maintained for more than 10 minutes, which, coincidentally, was the maximum length of a standard YouTube clip at the time. One FEI steward usually had to watch several riders at once, so the rules were now less enforceable than ever. Carl Jung once wrote that 'People will do anything, no matter how absurd, to avoid facing their own souls.' It seems equestrian federations will do anything, no matter how absurd, to avoid enforcing their own rules.

The international equestrian press lit up with headlines proclaiming that the FEI had banned hyperflexion. In fact, all the FEI had done was give it a new name. A short-term solution, if ever there was one, for a federation in need of patching up its public image.

8

Equestrian sport and media repression

'Olympic principles are United Nations principles', UN Secretary General Ban Ki-moon famously said during the 2009 Olympic Congress in Copenhagen. But while the FEI remains part of the Olympic family, that statement is only partially true. Whilst the UN puts a strong emphasis on press freedom and 'Information as a Public Good', equestrian sport stakeholders rely on harassment, intimidation and vexatious litigation to silence their critics and hide the truth.

THE FIRST SIGNIFICANT THING TO happen after the FEI had pretended to ban hyperflexion in February 2010, was that Anky van Grunsven sued the equestrian news website, Eurodressage, and its owner, Flemish journalist Astrid Appels, for defamation. Appels had used an archive photo of one of Mrs van Grunsven's Olympic horses to illustrate a news story about the FEI's announcement regarding hyperflexion. Mrs Van Grunsven, who claimed to practise the benign and entirely unrelated technique called LDR, took exception to being connected with rollkur or hyperflexion, and sued. The case generated more international interest and support for Ms Appels than Mrs van Grunsven had perhaps anticipated, and the lawsuit was eventually retracted. In addition to the lawsuit, Ms Appels said she had also been harassed by Mrs van Grunsven's husband, Sjef Janssen, via email. He had allegedly called the journalist a 'super bitch', 'totally deranged' and 'a tiny, miserable figure'.[1]

'The riders don't feel comfortable with the camera'

When the next FEI World Cup qualifier in Odense came along in October 2010, Luise and I went to document how the application of LDR was going without the use of 'aggressive force'. We had not been filming long before we were approached by an Olympic medallist who told us we were not allowed to record video. We told him we were journalists and had press accreditation, and he rode off again. Shortly after, we were contacted by a man wearing a jacket with the logo of the show organisers. He did not introduce himself, but when Luise asked if he was a steward, he said yes. The man told us that we were not allowed to film by the barrier around the warm-up arena. We had to stand back three metres because we were making the riders feel unsafe. 'They can't make the horses go the way they want them to, so you have to move back', said the man. Luise asked what her filming had to do with the riders not being able to make their horses go as they wanted them to, but her question remained unanswered. The man just insisted that we had to move back, so we did.

The next day we used a small consumer camera in case it was the size of our equipment that was the undisclosed reason for our presence bothering the riders. We had not been there for long when the mystery man came back. I had gone to the bathroom, so Luise had to face him alone. He repeated his request for us to stand back several metres from the barrier. When Luise asked him what the problem was, he said: 'The problem is that they find it irritating. Or the horses find it irritating. I don't know.' Luise then explained that we were using a small camera

1 Astrid Appels, 'Anky van Grunsven Sues Eurodressage', Eurodressage, 25 Aug 2010, https://www.eurodressage.com/2010/08/25/anky-van-grunsven-sues-eurodressage, accessed 22 Aug 2021.

specifically to avoid bothering the horses. Much bigger cameras than ours were present by the barrier. Why were we the only ones who had to move back? Luise told the man that she could not do her job as an accredited journalist unless she could stand by the barrier. The man said he didn't care. He represented the organisers and they wanted her to stand back. Raising his voice and questioning Luise's intelligence, the official then threatened to have guards come and remove us, regardless of our press accreditation, if we did not comply.

The FEI chief steward, Jaana Alvesparr, also got involved. Luise kept the tape rolling through these conversations, so I can tell you very exactly what was said. You can also watch the video on YouTube. It's called 'FEI Officials at Work'.[2]

Luise: 'What I see is a man harassing a journalist for doing her job.'

FEI Chief Steward Jaana Alvesparr: 'Yes, I can see that too, but that is not the problem. The problem is that the riders don't feel comfortable with the camera.'

We kept filming by the barrier for the rest of the day and were not thrown out. But we did decide it wasn't worth it getting press accreditation in the future.

FEI World Reining Finals: well that was awkward

In the spring of 2011, I was asked by several people to go and film at an FEI reining show. What dressage is to cavalry riding, reining is to livestock herding traditions. A now useless, highly stylised imitation of something that once had a practical purpose. Nobody who actually relied on their horse's soundness or sanity for their survival would ever put that horse through anything like FEI dressage or reining.

I had never been to a reining show, and this was the FEI World Reining

2 Epona TV, 'FEI Officials at Work', YouTube video, 28 June 2011, https://www.youtube.com/watch?v=n99uFM4XCs8.

Finals in Sweden. The top prize was USD 100,000 and the title of World Reining Champion. Luise was away, so I went with my neighbour. We had no press accreditation, so we just bought tickets and went to sit in the indoor arena where the warm-up was going on.

It has never been so easy to film rollkur. The riders seemed proud of their riding. I got a polite hat tip and a 'howdy' from one man as he incriminated himself in front of my rolling camera. He would later threaten to sue us for publishing that footage. Riders often imagine that their riding looks very different than the objective reality, and when they see the images or footage for which they gladly posed, they feel betrayed by the photographer.

At the FEI World Reining Finals, stewards sat in high chairs like tennis umpires. One of them was FEI Honorary Steward General for Reining, Eric Straus: the highest-ranking FEI reining steward in the world. Mr Straus is also a jumping steward and fulfilled that role at the Rio Olympic Games in 2016.

There was plenty of rollkur at the FEI World Reining Final, but other questionable techniques were applied as well. Some of them were new to me. One of the things reining horses have to do is called a sliding stop. The horse is brought to a fast gallop and then has to stop very abruptly, which causes them to skid on their hind legs. There are special horse shoes for this, and the practice is a common cause of injury to reining horses. Riders were practicing the sliding stop by galloping their horses straight at a wall and only allowing them to stop at the last minute. A couple of times, they left it too late and the horse slid into the barrier. At no time while this was going on did the stewards intervene.

Another reining move is the spin, in which the horse has to demonstrate the ability to turn fast on the haunches. One rider made her horse spin and spin and spin. Every time it seemed like she would stop, she made the horse spin another 360 degrees. These riders made Patrik Kittel look like Jane Goodall. Even though we were indoors, my companion put on her sunglasses, to hide the fact that she had tears in her eyes. The FEI stewards drank coffee and looked at their phones.

When I arrived home and loaded the footage and started sending it to Luise, we quickly realised we had another major scandal on our hands. Prior to publishing the FEI World Reining Final footage, I sent it to the FEI department of communications to ask the usual question: was this riding in accordance with the FEI Code of Conduct?

This is the response I received from the FEI: 'Representatives from FEI HQ spoke to the Chief Steward in Bökebergs Gård and were assured that all practice sessions were fully monitored, that each training session was timed and that all practices were within the rules that are currently in place.'[3]

Again, the YouTube videos went viral. This time, even faster than they had with the blue tongue incident, because we now had quite an international following. Another rider threatened to sue us for publishing the footage of how he had prepared his horse. As before, the FEI legal department asked for our raw footage. As before, we told the FEI it was not our problem if its stewards were not enforcing its rules. If the FEI wanted to know what had been done to horses at the FEI World Reining Finals, it could ask its Honorary Steward General Eric Straus whose presence could be clearly ascertained from the footage, due to the prominence of the stewards' chairs in the arena.

On 1 August 2011, the FEI issued a press release announcing the completion of its inquiry into the World Reining Final. By now, the story had changed, so that, according to the FEI, multiple 'verbal warnings' had been issued during the event for various offences, 'including riding for too long, running a horse into the wall, overly aggressive use of the hands, overly aggressive use of the spurs and attempting to train post-competition.'[4] The press release also claimed that no further action

3 FEI department of Communications, email to author, 23 May 2011.

4 FEI, 'FEI Reining Committee agrees new rule structure', media update, 1 Aug 2011, https://inside.fei.org/media-updates/fei-reining-committee-agrees-new-

could be taken against the offending riders 'due to the lack of authenticated evidence such as original unedited video footage'. In other words, the FEI can't protect horses against aggressive riding unless a spectator or journalist happens to document it and is willing to hand over their raw footage. At the same time, FEI show organisers are making it more and more difficult to record video footage at their events.

This time, the FEI really did change its rules. It banned the practice of riding horses into the wall and put a cap on the number of consecutive spins allowed in the warm-up. But it was never announced whether the apparent use of 'aggressive force' had any consequences for the riders or stewards involved. Two of the riders in our footage had won medals, including the world title. Those results quietly disappeared from the FEI database. Normally, when a rider is disqualified from an FEI event for abusing their horse or for any other reason, that result is still listed in the database. If you look up the history of the athletes involved in the World Reining Finals scandal, all their results can be seen in the FEI database, except the ones from that day. It's as if it never happened.

'Take down that video!'

In 2012 Patrik Kittel was photographed subjecting Scandic to some LDR at the London Olympics. German photographer Julia Rau captured the act and published the photos, and outrage ensued as many fans suddenly realised just how much LDR looked like the rollkur they had been told the FEI no longer allowed. The FEI's Facebook page was inundated with angry posts. The federation assured fans that the photos showed only 'a moment in time'. The welfare of the horse was paramount, the FEI posted on Facebook. 'We are aware that there is concern about some training methods, but photographs can be misleading. Rest assured that our stewards are always there, on the ground, monitoring all training

---

rules-structure, accessed 4 Oct 2021.

sessions. We are on the case.'[5] This post and its many angry comments from horse lovers is still available on Facebook.

Luise and I had not been planning to go to the London Olympics, but the claims by the FEI that Julia Rau's photos didn't represent reality, because they were only moments in time, cried out for a bit of investigative video journalism. We had no tickets or accreditation, and chances we would get any footage were slim to none. We still decided to go. While strolling through the park in Greenwich, we came across a 'satellite' schooling arena. It was far away from the main complex of the equestrian events and the fence was covered in pink fabric making it difficult to see what was going on. Nonetheless, it was clear that some horses were being schooled.

A guard patrolled the perimeter, shooing away curious onlookers. One fan was threatened by him for taking a photo of her idol over the fence, even after having asked for and obtained the rider's permission. The guard told the fan that the riders' 'rivals' were not to know how they were training, and that this was why there was so much secrecy. He told her she could get 'banned from the whole Olympics' if anybody reported her for taking pictures of the practice arena. One must assume that the riders' rivals were all on the same side of the pink mesh as they were, so the guard's excuse for threatening the fan made little sense, but he seemed to believe in it himself.

Lengthy, high quality footage was not necessary for debunking the claims by the FEI that Julia Rau's photos were misleading. All that needed to be documented was that horses were deliberately put into the posture which had sparked the scandal. Once we had found a vantage point from which we could film over the fence, that was easy. We uploaded the

5 FEI, 'The FEI absolutely condemns all cruel or aggressive training methods', Facebook post, 5 Aug 2012, https://www.facebook.com/the.fei/posts/402040016510063?comment_id=402103173170414, accessed 22 Aug 2021.

footage to YouTube, which was like pouring petrol on a fire. Of course, you already know this story. You are the IOC, and you had your lawyer, Frédérique Reynertz, threaten us with legal action unless we took down the video. That's how incriminating it was. We had to get the Danish Union of Journalists and the National Union of Journalists in the UK on the case to make your counsel understand that you were in the wrong. The national Danish newspapers picked up the story: 'Olympic overlords threaten Danish journalists'.[6]

I'm sure you weren't trying to be bullies, but that's how you came across. For as long as Equestrian is part of the Olympic Games, the FEI will continue to put you in that situation. The FEI has no choice. Hiding the truth about how horses are ridden at FEI competitions is the only way to maintain the appearance that the federation governs horse sport with integrity. In a world of smartphones and social media, this task will prove impossible.

Intimidation of photographers at shows

In 2013, the FEI ECCO European Dressage Championships were held in Denmark, and Luise and I were joined at the fence around the warm-up arena by animal rights activists. There was also a demonstration outside with protesters who had dyed their tongues blue and were sticking them out at ticket holders as they arrived. By this time, Luise and I felt that our presence at FEI horse shows was obsolete. We had shown people what was allowed to go on. What else was there to do, apart from allowing them to make up their own minds about whether or not they wanted to have anything to do with a sport where horses are treated the way they are treated by the FEI?

6 Thor Carlskov, 'Olympiske magtmænd truer danske journalister' [Olympic overlords threaten Danish journalists], *Ekstra Bladet*, 14 Aug 2012, https://ekstrabladet.dk/sport/anden_sport/anden_sport/article4016413.ece, accessed 22 Aug 2021.

The trouble with such a decision is that once you have published footage or photos of controversial riding, you become a magnet for people with photos or footage of controversial riding. They know you are not afraid to put it out there, so they come to you with their evidence, hoping you will make it public on their behalf. In 2014, we received 50 very disturbing photos from a private stallion show hosted by an Olympic medal-winning dressage rider. The photos clearly showed another blue tongue, belonging to a horse named Akeem, but the photographer had previously experienced intimidation when taking pictures at horse shows and so they did not want to be named. We agreed to publish the photos. This caused another major international equestrian scandal. The Danish newspapers which ran the story extraordinarily published it in English as well as Danish, because of the international interest it generated. The rider was even prosecuted for animal cruelty, but because the photographer did not wish to be named or to testify, the photographic evidence was deemed inadmissible in court, and the rider was acquitted. The Danish Equestrian Federation issued a warning to the rider for 'improper use of the bridle.' The FEI was silent.

In 2015, it happened again. A different photographer sent us photographs of the same rider who had been exposed the year before, this time competing at an FEI competition in Falsterbo in Sweden on a grey mare called Stamina. The rider's name is Andreas Helgstrand. He is a highly influential horse dealer and an Olympic medallist. His father is the President of the Danish Equestrian Federation. Mr Helgstrand is also an organiser of FEI competitions. In addition to the animal welfare angle, Andreas Helgstrand has hit the Danish tabloids several times when horse breeders have accused him of attempting to defraud them by lying about the sale price of horses he has brokered for them.[7] He has been

7 Silla Bakalus, 'Nye anklager mod toprytter: Ville snyde for millioner' [New accusations against top rider: wanted to cheat for millions], *B.T.*, 11 May 2014, https://www.bt.dk/krimi/nye-anklager-mod-toprytter-ville-snyde-for-millioner,

in the spotlight for underpaying a Romanian employee under what a professor in labour market conditions called 'slave like conditions.'[8] Mr Helgstrand said to the media at the time, that he did not think he had done anything wrong. 'People will work here for free just to be allowed to be here' he said. In 2015, Helgstrand was given a large fine for illegally employing an American rider.[9]

The very last thing Luise and I wanted at this point was another scandal revolving around Andreas Helgstrand. From the beginning, we have striven to hold the FEI accountable for the sort of riding it has allowed for decades to proliferate at its events. Individual riders cast as villains have the opposite effect. They serve as lighting rods for the rage and guilt of cognitively dissonant horse sport fans, who know deep down that something is very wrong, but aren't ready to admit it to themselves and cut ties with the sport. People can avoid holding the FEI and themselves accountable when there is a single, named individual they can hate instead.

But what are you going to do when you are the only media outlet in the world willing to publish these photos, with the means to get them out to an international equestrian audience? We published the photos under the headline 'Falsterbo Moments', and the result was predictable. In Denmark, the story was picked up by the tabloids, and it speaks to the grotesque nature of the photos that even FEI Secretary General Sabrina Zeender was forced to say something about them:

---

accessed 22 Aug 2021.

8 Silla Bakalus, 'OL-rytter i Lønskandale' [Olympic rider in wage scandal], *B.T.*, 12 Aug 2013, https://www.bt.dk/danmark/ol-rytter-i-loenskandale, accessed 22 Aug 2021.

9 Malte Nørgaard, 'Dansk dressurstjerne fik kæmpebøde for ulovlig arbejdskraft' [Danish dressage star received giant fine for illegal labour], *DR*, 18 Jan 2008, https://www.dr.dk/sporten/oevrig/dansk-dressurstjerne-fik-kaempeboede-ulovlig-arbejdskraft, accessed 22 Aug 2021.

> The FEI finds these images extremely disturbing. We are very concerned about this incident and we are investigating it thoroughly. We have already contacted the Chief Steward at Falsterbo to ask for a full report specifically on this issue, in addition to the normal event report that has already been sent to the FEI.[10]

Then, as usual, the FEI did nothing. What could it possibly do? No yellow cards had been given out during the show, which meant that no steward had seen any reason to intervene. What could be seen in the photographs was what was allowed by the FEI. The photographer offered to send all his material from the show, but the FEI ignored the offer.

The man who took the pictures is called Crispin Parelius Johannessen, and he is a British-Norwegian fine art photographer with a particular interest in how horses and equestrians are visually constructed in Western culture. Crispin holds two Master of Fine Arts degrees (one from St Martin's College and one from Goldsmiths at the University of London). Luise and I first met him at the FEI ECCO European Championships in 2013, where he was among the independent photographers standing next to us by the fence.

As an artist, Crispin directs his gaze at what others can't, or do not want to see. With his super sharp, high-resolution photographs, he strives to make the people looking at his art really notice what is being done to horses. He has shared with me his archive of incredibly detailed images and his frustration that people often reject them as lies, calling them 'moments in time' and refusing to accept them as documents of truth.

After the initial Falsterbo scandal had died down, Crispin and I remained in contact, and I produced a series of interviews with him,

---

10 Astrid Appels, 'Andreas Helgstrand Back in the Hot Seat after Publication Falsterbo Training Photos', Eurodressage, 27 Aug 2015, https://www.eurodressage.com/2015/08/27/andreas-helgstrand-back-hot-seat-after-publication-falsterbo-training-photos, accessed 22 Aug 2021.

in which he talks about the way the horse has been represented in art through the ages and the current wilful refusal to confront equine suffering in equestrian sport. If you want to watch the series, it's available on YouTube. It's called 'Equine images with Crispin Parelius Johannessen.'

Ahead of Falsterbo Horse Show in 2017, the organisers announced that the warm-up arenas would be monitored by video surveillance, to protect the riders against any photographs which had been 'taken out of context.' This was intriguing to me, because I knew that the photos, which riders and organisers were worried about, were not taken out of context. Would the organisers really release their surveillance footage in case of another scandal? I had to know, and so did Crispin. We decided to go together and to film and photograph the same riders at the same time. This way, we could combine the detail of Crispin's work with the context provided by my footage.

It had been four years since I had filmed at a horse show, and I had never been to Falsterbo. It was clear from the beginning that we were not welcome. Stewards were scowling at us and taking photos of us. Even seemingly random spectators walked up and photographed us with their phones, which, presumably, was supposed to bother us. We didn't mind because we were not doing anything wrong, but it was a little strange. From time to time, I took a break from filming with my big camera and live streamed a couple of minutes of the warm-up to Facebook from my phone. I did this to show people that it is not necessary to cherrypick 'moments in time' from hours of footage in order to show questionable riding. Such riding goes on all the time. It is the norm.

Late on the second day, I was contacted by a man I didn't know. He did not introduce himself, but claimed to be a representative of Swedish State Television (SVT). He said I was not allowed to live stream from the event because the rights to direct transmission were owned by SVT. This sounded odd to me because I had not streamed from the competition, and I was on a journalistic assignment, which I couldn't imagine SVT to have anything against. In fact, they had interviewed Luise in 2013 about our work and we had helped their cameraman to obtain the footage they needed for a news segment on rollkur.

The man would not show us any ID to document that he worked for SVT. I kept filming while I talked to him because he had not documented to me that he had the authority to tell me what to do. I informed him that I was a journalist doing my job, that I had not realised that SVT's live rights included the entire show ground and that I would not live stream any more snippets if they didn't want me to. SVT could get in touch later if they felt I had violated their rights. The man still insisted that I stop filming. I explained to him that I was not streaming, but recording footage for later use, and that this was my right. He said I wasn't to do that either. Then he called the on-site police and told them that we were filming and refusing to leave. At this point, we did not know his name and he had not shown us any ID. After the phone call, the man left. I kept filming and Crispin kept taking photographs.

We were joined by two horse owners. They told us we should be ashamed of ourselves, that we were morons and that it would be best for us if we were removed by security, because who knew what might happen otherwise, if a bunch of them got together? While they were saying this, the FEI steward was standing close to us. We thought she might have something to say to the men harassing a spectator and a member of the press, but that wasn't why she was there. She had recognised Crispin and was pointing her finger at him and warning him not to publish any photos with her in them without her approval.

Shortly after, the strange man returned with two police officers. We were told that they would confiscate our camera equipment if we didn't leave immediately. Crispin's too, even though he was there in his own right and had not published any of his photos yet. I told one of the officers that I had a right to document what was going on in the warm-up arena and that this was part of an ongoing, investigative work of journalism, but he just told me to take it up with the European Court of Human Rights. As we already had plenty of material and didn't want to risk losing any of it while our cameras were confiscated, we agreed to leave.

The man who refused to identify himself later turned out to be head of security for the show. His name is Carl-Magnus Olofsson. He does not work for SVT. SVT did not ask him to have us thrown out or even to tell us to stop filming. I contacted them once I arrived home, and they knew nothing of the incident. Other media outlets had been live streaming from the show that year. Some even streamed the competitions in the main arena, but we were the only ones whom security saw fit to have escorted off the premises by police.

When we arrived back home, we published some photos and footage from Falsterbo and suggested to the FEI that they publish the footage from their surveillance cameras to prove to the public that our documentation was false. They never did. I cut a 15-minute video segment about our adventures and published it on our website. We made it free to make sure it was seen by as many people as possible. Within a day of posting, it had been shared over 60,000 times on Facebook. It crashed our site, so in the end we uploaded it to YouTube instead. You can see it there if you like. It's called 'Farewell Falsterbo'.

This was the summer of 2017, when I also broke the de-nerving stories. It was then I decided I was done with horse sport. My original intent in going into equestrian journalism was to make the sport better. Luise and I both thought that we could help save Equestrian from extinction by providing some much-needed transparency and accountability through critical journalism, in order to force the FEI to wake up and begin to govern its sport. That summer, the penny finally dropped. The FEI would never do that, because it was no longer possible. The sport was too far gone and anyway, the world was leaving it behind.

Nowadays, it isn't even necessary to film riders and publish the footage in order to cause a rollkur scandal. The practice of hyperflexion is now so normalised and accepted in FEI circles that riders and even officials film and publish it themselves as examples of best practice.

Taking the fight to the courts

In May 2019, the French international FEI dressage judge, Isabelle Judet, inadvertently landed herself at the centre of a rollkur scandal when she hosted a dressage training session which was filmed and published on YouTube in order to promote her business. At times, the horses' necks got very short, leading critics to say that the video was promoting hyperflexion. One of these critics, an equine veterinarian named Eva Van Avermaet, posted links to the videos on her Facebook page, highlighting the riding, which she considered to be unhealthy for the horse.

As a dressage judge of international renown, Isabelle Judet did not like to be accused of promoting rollkur, a technique now defined by the FEI as abuse of the horse. Yet, she had chosen to publish footage of her horse, ridden by her daughter, in postures which occasionally matched to perfection the rollkur silhouette as defined in the FEI's manuals. In a perhaps ill-advised decision, Ms Judet took Dr Van Avermaet to court in June 2021 seeking EUR 18,000 in financial compensation for economic and moral damages. She also requested a court decision ordering Dr Van Avermaet to publish a press release with a statement that she had been criminally convicted of defamation of Ms Judet.

On 10 Jun 2021, the criminal tribunal of Vannes (Brittany, France) declared the direct summons by Ms Judet against Dr Van Avermaet null and void because the accusation of defamation was not substantiated by any clear or precise examples of the defamatory statements allegedly made by Dr Van Avermaet. Ms Judet was ordered to pay Dr Van Avermaet EUR 1,500 to cover her legal costs.

In a written statement based on his analysis of the case, law Professor Dr Dirk Voorhoof from the Human Rights Centre of Gent University, who specialises in media law and freedom of expression, called the lawsuit a clear case of Strategic Litigation Against Public Participation (SLAPP). Professor Voorhoof is a member of the European Centre for Press and Media Freedom (ECPMF) as well as CASE.EU, the Coalition against SLAPPS in Europe.

> 'The criminal complaint and legal action by Pamfou Dressage and Isabelle Judet against Eva Van Avermaet can undoubtedly be considered as a SLAPP (Strategic Litigation against Public Participation), a form of abusive use of the judiciary with the aim to intimidate, harass or silence a critical voice that took part in public debate or revealed illegal or unethical practices by institutions, public persons, corporate organisations or private persons.'[11]

By now, the news will have reached you that the Swiss animal rights organisation Wild beim Wild has pressed criminal charges against the IOC and the FEI for a string of alleged animal cruelty incidents, including several which took place during Tokyo 2020 and were televised.[12] There is no hiding from this problem. Horse abuse is now so embedded in equestrian sport that the FEI itself and its members are blind to it and therefore document and publish it themselves.

---

11 Professor emeritus Dr Dirk Voorhoof, Statement on SLAPP (Strategic Litigation gainst Public Participation) in the case of Pamfou Dressage and Isabelle Judet v. Eva Van Avermaet at the occasion of the judgement of the tribunal of Vannes (France) of 10 June 2021, email attachment from Eva Van Avermaet to Julie Taylor (authenticity verified by JT), sent 24 Aug 2021.

12 Wild beim Wild, 'Strafanzeige gegen IOC und FEI' [Criminal complaint against IOC and FEI], 16 Aug 2021, https://wildbeimwild.com/kampagnen/strafanzeige-gegen-ioc-und-fei/49553/2021/08/16/, accessed 22 Aug 2021.

If the IOC wants to be a driver—not an object—of change, now may be the time to cut Equestrian loose. Horses do not belong in the modern Olympic Games. I think you already know this, but for some reason, you have been unable so far to pull the trigger. I am writing this book to make sure that you know what I know.

9

The price of more flags is declining safety

Universality is a fundamental Olympic value, but it doesn't mix with equestrian sport. Making insufficiently experienced riders compete in jumping or the cross-country leg of eventing doesn't just humiliate them. It puts their lives at risk. The FEI has promised you to deliver 'more flags'. It has fulfilled that promise by compromising the fundamental value of Olympism, which is athlete safety.

I HAVE ALREADY TOUCHED ON the FEI's efforts to project globality but this topic deserves more discussion because not only is FEI sport not global, it cannot be global. Let us go back to the International Jumping Riders Club meeting in Rotterdam in 2019 where the president of the German Equestrian Federation defined the majority of national equestrian federations affiliated with the FEI as 'non-riding'. At that meeting, several prominent Olympic riders were accusing the FEI of steamrolling them in the decision making about the new jumping format, which was set to have its Olympic debut in Tokyo. The riders did not want this format, where teams are reduced from four to three riders, but the FEI had continuously insisted to them that it was the price they had to pay for remaining in the Olympic Games. The IOC wanted more flags but not more horses. This meant fewer horses per nation. The old format allowed each team of four to drop their worst score. Now all scores would count, which would put more pressure on riders, not to mention horses. Nations which would otherwise have been unable to qualify teams for Equestrian would now gain access to the competition. This is another dilemma for the FEI: the more global the sport is made to appear, the lower the criteria for Olympic qualification must be, which reduces the level of excellence at the Games. And the level of safety.

Logistical barriers limit opportunities to qualify

There is no solution to this problem on the immediate horizon. Aside from the economic barrier to entry, there are serious biosecurity issues involved when horses travel internationally, and they cannot easily be moved across national borders in every part of the world. Many countries have quarantine rules which make the kind of international competition circuits seen in Europe and North America impossible to organise. For instance, if a rider from South Africa wants to take part in a competition in Europe, their horse will currently have to be in quarantine in Mauritius for a minimum of three months. Riders wishing to go to the US for competitions must quarantine their horses for 60 days on arrival. During this quarantine, the horse must be kept inside at all times, under strict biosecurity measures. This is to prevent the spread of African Horse Sickness (AHS). It is not surprising that the only South African rider qualified for Tokyo lives in Germany.

The World Organisation for Animal Health (OIE) publishes a list of countries which are deemed free of AHS, and most of Africa is not on that list. AHS is a highly deadly, species-hopping viral disease (for horses, the mortality rate ranges from 70 to 95 percent) which can affect donkeys, mules, zebra, and even camels, in addition to horses. Antibodies have also been found in dogs and elephants. In other words, this is a disease which poses a tangible threat to communities which have yet to industrialise and where people still rely on working animals for food production and transport. The virus is transmitted by bloodsucking midges, and in the first quarter of 2020, an unprecedented outbreak occurred in Thailand, killing hundreds of horses and causing the country to lose its ASH-free status. For the owners of racehorses and sport horses, such an outbreak is upsetting and expensive (even if the existing quarantine rules are even more expensive in terms of lost revenue). For rural subsistence farming communities that rely on horses and ponies for their survival, the consequences of an ASH outbreak can be devastating. The work to produce a safe and effective vaccine is still ongoing, and working equids don't tend to live in stables which can easily be midge-proofed. For these reasons—and more—the rules in place to prevent spread of the disease are very strict.

The FEI, along with the racing industry, has been lobbying for years for the de-regulation of horse exports from affected areas, claiming that 'high health, high performance' horses should be exempt from the strict rules which limit the export of equines from geographical areas where the virus is endemic. Whether the COVID-19 pandemic has done such plans any good remains to be seen. But for the time being, riders in large parts of the world are unable to travel with their horses.

There is a reason why FEI Jumping had to stage the Tokyo 2020 Olympic qualifying event for Asia Pacific in the Netherlands. There is a reason why nobody on the Olympic jumping team from New Zealand actually lives in New Zealand. There is a reason why the three riders whose results qualified Egypt's jumping team for Tokyo were based in California, Northern Ireland, and Belgium. And there is a reason why the five top ranking Australian jumping riders don't live in Australia. If you really want to make it in equestrian sport, you have to be where the big competitions are.

In 2019, there were 23,300 European FEI athletes registered to compete in the three Olympic equestrian disciplines. For the entire rest of the world combined, that number was 10,438. The figure for Europe does not even include all the riders who are registered with federations outside Europe but must live there in order to compete. Like Sri Lanka's only FEI rider, who grew up in Sweden and lives in Germany. Or Palestine's only dressage contender, a middle-aged German man who made it to Rio 2016 after obtaining dual citizenship between his birth country and the State of Palestine, but continues to reside in Germany. These people count as athletes outside of Europe, even though they are based in European countries, and there are more like them. For instance, India's only Tokyo-qualified rider—based in Germany—and the entire Japanese Olympic jumping team and most of the dressage and eventing riders: all based in either the UK, the Netherlands or Germany. What you measure is what you'll get. If you ask the FEI for more flags, you'll get more flags. Actual universality in horse sport is a pipe dream.

The vast over-representation of European and Europe-based riders in FEI sport is not something for FEI Solidarity to deal with by going to Sub-Saharan Africa to train more officials to increase capacity. In Europe and North America, where FEI competitions are most common and run smoothly, the ratios of officials to athletes are 0.17 and 0.18, respectively. For all the Sub-Saharan African nations combined, the total number of athletes registered to compete in Olympic disciplines in 2019 was 198. The number of officials for the same region was 240.

Standards in Equestrian's 'new markets' are still too low

China is not known for its shortage of athletic talent, and the nation's equestrian federation has been affiliated with the FEI for 38 years. Yet, on 31 July 2021, the best Chinese jumping rider was listed as number 1033 in the FEI World Rankings. When China qualified its jumping team for

Tokyo, the riders were all riding ready-made Grand Prix horses trained in Europe by European riders. Nobody even bothered to change the horses' nationalities or ownership in the FEI database, until after China's Olympic qualification was confirmed. At the 1* (1* represents the lowest tier of FEI competitions, with 5* being the highest) designated qualifier event in Valkenswaard, Holland, the Chinese team accumulated 47 faults between them. This result was later used by Olympic medal-winning rider and FEI Jumping Committee member Cian O'Connor as an example that the FEI is dumbing down the sport to make it appear more universal than it really is.

At the IJRC General Assembly in Rotterdam in 2019, Mr O'Connor had this to say to FEI President Ingmar De Vos: 'Modernisation has to take place with the countries being up to the level. You say we're modernising to take more countries, yet some of the qualifications are a joke.'[1] Mr O'Connor also accused President De Vos and Jumping Committee Chairman, Stephan Ellenbruch, of being false and disingenuous about how the new jumping format had come about. Riders did not feel they had been heard by the FEI. 'There's no point consulting if you ignore. That's not consulting. That's just dictatorship and that's what has gone on.' In an impassioned statement to President De Vos, Mr. O'Connor proceeded to accuse the FEI of also mismanaging the non-Olympic, international competitions in the name of false inclusivity:

> You have made the product so weak that no-one wants to go. The course builders are building it too small. The FEI is in disarray and you need to wake up to see it. Twenty, thirty years ago it was full of people who knew something about the sport. Now it's administrators. If you don't realise that the thing is a total sinking ship, you are deluded.

Mr. O'Connor proceeded to invoke the Olympic qualification results of the Pan American Games as another example that jumping was being

1 International Jumping Riders Club, Video stream of panel debate.

dumbed down. 'In Lima, three weeks ago, the team that was fourth had forty-two faults or something. The next team had sixty faults. How is that comparable to when they get to the Olympic Games?' Mr O'Connor demanded to know.[2]

The team which placed fifth at the Pan American Games was Argentina. Between them, the riders racked up 62.19 faults, which was not originally sufficient for an Olympic qualification. But after Canada's Nicole Walker failed her doping test and was disqualified, the Canadian team result slipped from fourth to seventh, and Argentina was able to take its place in Tokyo.

As of July 2021, countries like Belgium, Switzerland and the USA could pick their entire Olympic jumping teams from the world's top 20 riders. Two out of Morocco's three jumping athletes are not even in the world top 500. In eventing, five nations dominate the world top 20, whereas the highest performing Thai eventing rider ranks as number 281.

Contrived universality may harm athlete safety and public opinion

It's normal for countries with less experience in a sport to field athletes without a chance of winning a medal at the Olympic Games. After all, sport is first and foremost about taking part. But this presents a real problem in disciplines which are potentially dangerous to riders and horses if they are over-faced by the courses they meet at the Olympic Games.

The course builders have to make the sport easier, to make it safe for riders who are nowhere near the level of the international elite. If courses are built for the best riders to have an honest sporting competition at the Olympic Games, less advanced riders and their horses will be at risk. There may even be horse falls and catastrophic injuries (both of which occurred in Tokyo), and it is all going to be televised to the world,

2 International Jumping Riders Club, Video stream of panel debate.

potentially causing irreparable harm to the public image of the sport and the riders. From the perspective of the best Olympic riders, what they faced in Tokyo was set to be either a charade of a competition or a high risk of a public animal cruelty scandal.

As it happened, Singapore's only equestrian in Tokyo, the dressage rider Caroline Chew (based in the United Kingdom) left the dressage arena in tears after the judge at C had rung the bell and stopped her because her horse was bleeding from the mouth. Sri Lanka's Mathilda Karlsson (based in Germany, represented Sweden until 2018, and qualified for Tokyo under highly controversial circumstances)[3] was eliminated in the very first class after her horse refused to jump. Israel's Teddy Vlock (a dual citizen based in the US who switched to competing for Israel in 2018) looked dangerously over-horsed from the beginning of the jumping team qualifier on Amsterdam 27, a horse he purchased in January 2021. Amsterdam—originally part of the team which qualified Canada for the Tokyo Olympics—refused at the second fence, and later suffered a fall when his rider lost his balance over a jump and the pair came crashing down on top of the obstacle. It's unlikely the humiliation of these athletes at the Olympic Games in Tokyo did much to promote grassroots equestrian sport in the countries they represent.

The Thai riders in Tokyo were also let down by the new format. There are known factors which contribute to the likelihood of horse falls during the dangerous cross-country stage of eventing. Horses are in greater peril of falling at the highest level of competition and at championships. An inadequately experienced rider also adds to the risk. In 2015–16, an independent audit of eventing safety was compiled for the FEI; one of its recommendations was to exclude less-accomplished riders from

3 European US Asian Equine Lawyers, 'Mathilda Karlsson's successful appeal to the CAS against the FEI', 20 May 2021, https://www.europeanequinelawyers.com/mathilda-karlssons-successful-appeal-to-the-cas-against-the-fei/, accessed 12 Sep 2021.

competing at the highest level, for their safety and that of their horses.[4]

The FEI divides eventing riders into four categories, according to their prior achievements in the discipline: A, B, C, and D. As of July 2021, the Thailand Equestrian Federation had a total of four riders registered to compete in the discipline of eventing at FEI level. Three of them represented their country at the Tokyo Olympics. Two of them were classed in category C and one in category D. None of these riders had ever competed at the highest level before. Neither had any of their horses. As predicted by the FEI's own report, the lowest ranked rider's horse fell at one of the first obstacles of the cross-country event. Another rider fell off his horse. The third Thai rider was disqualified because his horse refused to jump. Including an eventing team of intermediate riders from a nation where eventing is in no way established doesn't just endanger the athletes and horses. It makes a mockery of the Olympic ideal of excellence. The FEI would have known this all along. It would have been a conscious choice to ignore the risks in favour of adding another flag.

In an attempt to ensure the safety of such athletes and horses, the FEI invented a new and reduced level of difficulty for Tokyo, called 'Olympic'. At 'Olympic' level, demands are reduced for the cross-country phase, compared with the world's most prestigious horse trials, such as Badminton and Kentucky. As we now know, even reducing the level of difficulty was not enough to keep all athletes and horses safe. But even if it had been, surely it is not desirable for sports to have to dumb themselves down for the Olympic Games?

At the IJRC meeting in Rotterdam, four times Olympic jumping gold medallist Ludger Beerbaum asked FEI President De Vos whether the FEI could not have been more transparent with the IOC in explaining these

4 FEI, 'An Audit into Eventing Incorporating an Analysis of Risk Factors for Cross Country Horse Falls at FEI Eventing Competitions', 26 July 2016, 10, https://inside.fei.org/system/files/Eventing%20Audit%20-%20Charles%20Barnett%20-%20Final%20Report%2026.07.16.pdf, accessed 22 Aug 2021.

unique challenges that face Equestrian in trying to comply with Olympic Agenda 2020. 'Maybe much more should have been done to say, "hey, we have a problem here. It's not so easy!" Explain this to the technical bodies in the IOC. Say, "we have limits to how open and flexible we can be!"'

Mr. Beerbaum was right, of course. Equestrian sport does have limits to how open and flexible it can be. That is the elephant in the room. Horses are already pushed beyond their limits, so that they need controversial drugs even to function. Rio 2016 saw four disqualifications for abuse of the whip and spurs. That's 5.7 percent of entries. The reason, according to President of the Ground Jury, Stephan Ellenbruch, was the high stakes of the Olympic Games. 'We see that riders are under very much pressure here ... Maybe they are over-using their spurs a little bit, or even their whip,' Mr. Ellenbruch said to Reuters at the time.[5]

Equestrian is not a global sport, and the pretence is killing the very thing the FEI claims to safeguard. What is actually being safeguarded with these new formats are the sweet jobs of administrators in Lausanne. To protect the sport would have been for the FEI to accept four or five decades ago that it is not suitable for television and will never appeal to a mass market. That ship has now sailed.

The Swiss Olympic gold medallist, Steve Guerdat, who is one of the highest-ranked jumping riders in the world, publicly washed his hands of the new Olympic jumping format at the IJRC meeting in Rotterdam. He had this to say to President De Vos: 'There was no compromise through it all. I think you have to take responsibility. Nowhere do I want to read that there was a compromise between the FEI and riders for the mess that we are going to see in Tokyo.'

---

5 Caroline Stauffer, 'Equestrian: Four show jumpers disqualified by "blood rule"', Reuters, 17 Aug 2016, https://www.reuters.com/article/us-olympics-rio-equestrian-jumpingteam-b-idUSKCN10S27Y, accessed 12 Sep 2021.

10

The equestrian fanbase is overstated

Many 'fans' of Equestrian have very little interest in the details of the sport, and are really only interested in the horses. Meanwhile, increasing public awareness of animal welfare issues turns former genuine fans away.

THE FEI WILL TELL YOU that it has a global fanbase of 750 million people. This number is based on research conducted by the consultancy firm, Intelligent Research in Sponsoring (IRIS), on behalf of the FEI. The number is surprisingly high, considering that the FEI's main Facebook page had just over a million fans, and @fei_global had less than half a million followers on Instagram and less than 90,000 on Twitter in July 2020. But this is not the only interesting thing about the research.

According to the map of global fans presented to the FEI by Managing Director of IRIS, Peter Weber, over half of the global equestrian fan base appears to be in China. At first glance, it looks as if IRIS has conducted its survey in the bar at the Macau Jockey Club. China had 645 registered FEI athletes in 2019. With a population of 1.4 billion people, that amounts to a participation rate of 0.00005 percent. However, the small print on the IRIS map clears up any confusion by explaining that the term 'equestrian fan' refers to any person willing to say that they are 'at least a little interested' in equestrian sport.

The horse is a powerful symbol in many cultures, so asking people in a nation with little or no equestrian activity in the Olympic disciplines whether they are at all interested in horse sport, risks generating a lot of false positives, because the question may easily be understood as: 'are you at least a little bit interested in horses?' A lot of people are interested in horses. Even more people are at least a little bit interested in horses. This does not necessarily mean they are going to be fans of horse sport. You cannot assume that everyone who loves dogs is going to want to fund greyhound racing. The opposite is probably more likely, once the dog lovers find out what greyhound racing entails. Even Mr Weber's global map of equestrian fans states (in the small print) that the results for China should be 'interpreted carefully in terms of social desirability'.

In support of my hunch that people with little or no experience of equestrian sport are more likely to say they are fans, the lowest levels of interest were generally found by IRIS in the countries with the highest level of participation. Sweden has a population of 10,230,000 citizens and 973 active, registered FEI athletes (2019). This participation rate works out at 0.009 percent, and even this is the highest of any country included in the research commissioned by the FEI. In Sweden, the percentage of respondents qualified as 'fans' represented the lowest level of interest anywhere. New Zealand, which had the second highest FEI participation rate at 0.008 percent, yielded the second lowest level of interest. It is difficult to imagine another sport where participation rates correlate inversely with spectator popularity. But, once you get your head around it, it is not so surprising that this should apply in the case of Equestrian.

The problem is that being a fan of Equestrian is turning out to be antithetical to being a lover of horses. The core target audience for the FEI consists of women who profess to care about animals. This presents a unique challenge for a federation whose product is animal exploitation and whose by-product is animal suffering and slaughter. In countries like Sweden and Great Britain, where rollkur, doping and other forms of abuse in FEI sport have been covered by national news media, people have a better understanding of what it means to say that they are fans of equestrian disciplines. Many now consider that it is the opposite of being a fan of horses. I am a good example of that. I am an upper-middle-class woman with a rural background. I live on a country property with horse facilities half an hour outside Copenhagen. I grew up competing in jumping and dressage, and my family was also involved with racing. However, here I am in 2021, completing a book about all the ways in which Equestrian does not belong in the Olympic Games or even the world. Faced with the choice between fairness to the horses and following the sport I grew up loving, I turned my back on the sport. I was not the first person to make this choice and I will be far from the last. There is a growing body of ex-equestrians with insider knowledge, who are willing to actively work to curtail the abuses of power by the FEI. They tend to be highly educated, socially connected and comparatively affluent—just like the FEI's demographic, because they were the FEI's demographic. PETA will be the least of the IOC's concerns, unless you cut the FEI loose.

Aside from the amount of research I have done, I am nothing out of the ordinary. The target audience for horse sport mostly likes horses first and sport second. The FEI knows this, and it is part of the reason why its social media interactions have picked up in recent years. The federation is deliberately posing as an organisation which is about horses in general, to lure in new followers, to whom it can then attempt to market its disciplines. Any uptick in digital interactions should be interpreted within this context. For example, let us compare the response to two posts shared two days apart on FEI Jumping's Facebook page. The first one, on 6 July 2020, was a link to a video feature about European jumping champion, Martin Fuchs: content specifically about jumping and one of the discipline's leading icons. In 12 days, it received five comments and 66 shares. The second link, posted two days later, was about the conservation efforts to protect the Exmoor Pony, a topic which is completely unrelated to FEI jumping except for the fact that equines are involved. In ten days, this post received 52 comments and 589 shares. The horses themselves are much more compelling than the sport.

In October 2018, FEI's commercial director, Ralph Straus, had this to say to SportsPro about the marketing strategy for horse sport:

> A lot of people are not necessarily interested in the top competitions, nor in the FEI as an organisation ...What they are interested in is the horse. That's something that, as an equestrian federation, we have in common with them. Therefore, in terms of our content, part of that has to be based around the top competitions, but we have also had to develop a new content strategy, with a lot of the content focused on the horse itself—things like travelling with horses, fashion for horses, medication, nutrition, the top places in the world to ride a horse. The focus has to be on the horse in order to engage with a wider fanbase.[1]

The problem with this approach is that scientific studies are casting more and more light on what is really going on in horse sport, and people who are primarily interested in horses are not going to be impressed. In 2018, a study published in the *Equine Veterinary Journal* showed that 9.3 percent of horses examined at equestrian competitions had oral lesions or blood in the corners of their mouths after taking part.[2] The risk of such injuries rose with the level of competition. The study only looked at injuries which could be diagnosed without examining the inside of the horse's mouth, so it is likely that the real prevalence of mouth injuries in

1 Nick Friend, 'From the horse's mouth: Ralph Straus on the commercial growth of equestrian's seven disciplines', SportsPro, 11 Oct 2018, https://www.sportspromedia.com/from-the-magazine/fei-equestrian-ralph-straus-commercial, accessed 22 Aug 2021.

2 M. Uldahl and H.M. Clayton, 'Lesions associated with the use of bits, nosebands, spurs and whips in Danish competition horses', *Equine Veterinary Journal*, 51/2 (2019), https://doi.org/10.1111/evj.12827.

competition horses is significantly higher. In our work, Luise and I have seen (and documented) lacerations of the lips in children's competition ponies. One does not need strong arms to injure a horse's mouth—just the will to win, and one of the many inventive bits permitted by the FEI and its member federations.

In 2020, Professor David J Mellor (the same professor of animal science who invented the Five Domains) published a review study of mouth pain in horses that sought to burst the bubble of what Professor Mellor calls 'bit blindness'.[3] This is the inability of equestrians and equestrian industry professionals to recognise the signs of bit-induced mouth pain in horses, due to the problem's widespread and normalised occurrence in equestrian sport.

Professor Mellor compares bit blindness to a condition, whereby dairy farmers think that their lame cows are sound, because they have so many sick animals that they have become used to seeing the symptoms of illness as normal. In both cases, the 'blindness' is problematic, because it leads people to ignore the suffering of animals for whom they are supposed to care. Professor Mellor first summarises the evidence that horses are able to consciously experience pain; and then the evidence that both acute and chronic mouth injuries result from the use of bits to control horses during equitation. He names the most common sites of bit-induced injuries—the lips and cheeks and the area of the horse's mandible where the bit acts directly on the gums—and points out that these areas are highly sensitive to pain:

> All oral sites referred to are richly supplied with nociceptors and are susceptible to bruising, laceration and ulceration. The prevalence of these injuries clearly indicates that, notwithstanding many riders' specific intentions to the contrary, rein tensions transmitted to the bit

3 David J Mellor, 'Mouth Pain in Horses: Physiological Foundations, Behavioural Indices, Welfare Implications, and a Suggested Solution', *Animals*, 10/4 (2020), 572. https://doi.org/10.3390/ani10040572

> may often cause tissue trauma and associated pain at intensities which are of welfare concern. Note, in addition, that the periosteal gums of the interdental space are especially sensitive to noxious stimulation. In fact, they are so sensitive that low bit pressures which would not produce detectable lesions can still cause significant pain, as indicated by the "Mellor pen test", and higher pressures that do produce visible lesions would cause marked to extremely severe pain.[4]

Nociceptors are pain receptors. The 'interdental space' refers to the area of the mandible most affected by the bit or bits. Horses naturally have a gap between their incisors and molars where there are no teeth. Equestrians call this site the 'bars of the mouth', and many bits are designed to put pressure on the gums there. Even bits designed to act solely on the horse's tongue commonly slip and act on the bars as well. The 'Mellor pen test' is a teaching exercise invented by Professor Mellor, which you can perform on yourself to get an idea of what it feels like for horses when riders apply pressures of several—sometimes over 40—kilograms per centimetre squared to their sensitive gums. Google the 'Mellor pen test' if you want to try it. Included on Professor Mellor's list of signs of bit-induced mouth pain are 'slightly open or gaping mouth' and 'nasal plane at or behind the vertical'. The same signs which FEI officials are supposed to monitor, but which are routinely rewarded with medals at the Olympic Games.

I came across the review as I was researching for this book, and I found myself repeatedly agreeing out loud with Professor Mellor's analysis. 'Bit blindness' is exactly what Luise and I have been trying to cure with our video work from the warm-up arenas at equestrian competitions. We just never had a name for it. We wanted to highlight what the horses are constantly expressing, which—if you'll excuse the anthropomorphism—is 'ouch, stop hurting us.' As Professor Mellor writes in his review, 'Once fully recognised … the signs of bit-induced mouth

4 Mellor, 'Mouth pain", 11.

pain in horses, as with lameness in dairy cows, cannot be "unseen".[5]

Initially, this inability to 'unsee' the signs of bit related pain and anxiety displayed by horses causes a desire in fans to petition the FEI to enforce its rules against abuse of the horse. But, since the FEI appears unwilling or unable to enforce these rules, many fans eventually give up and turn away from what now appears to them as outright animal cruelty. 'I can't watch anymore,' they say. And then they stop watching. This has already been happening in Europe and North America for some time, and should the FEI be successful in developing new markets, the same thing will happen there. People will want to know more about the horses who fascinate them, and they will discover the science, now readily available, which documents the pain and fear inflicted on those horses by the riding permitted in FEI sport.

The FEI is well aware of the perception of Equestrian as animal abuse. According to the Repucom survey commissioned by the FEI in 2014, this is especially challenging when marketing dressage. Problems such as 'media exposure', 'difficulty understanding the judging', 'boring to watch' and 'too expensive' will never go away, because they are all inherent to the discipline.

There is an obvious causal link between 'boring to watch' and 'media exposure'. Save the introduction of strobe lights and flame throwers, every gimmick has been tried to make dressage more interesting. The FEI has transformed it into an entirely different discipline, and people still don't want to watch it. Although innovations like freestyle to music and breeding horses with naturally extravagant movements have gained a few gasps of appreciation from an uninformed audience, it has lost the interest of people who genuinely understand the rules, because they don't consider it to be dressage. And those who don't understand the rules will quickly be disillusioned once they begin to know more and look past the arched necks and extravagant movements and begin to see the gaping

5 Mellor, 'Mouth Pain', 130.

jaws, the jerking hands, and learn that a horse with a swishing tail is far more likely to be showing distress than jauntily keeping the beat.

All that is left in the struggle to market dressage to the masses is to keep making the tests shorter and thereby more bearable to sit through. The obvious destination of this strategy is to drop the discipline entirely.

As discussed in Chapter 6, the judging is never going to get any easier to understand. Explanatory tools used in other sports will only make dressage more confusing for spectators, as judges inexplicably give medals to riders who don't fulfil any of the basic criteria listed in the rules, and whose horses are obviously in pain.

As more and more people overcome their bit blindness, jumping and eventing will experience problems as well, because horses in these disciplines also show signs of pain, which are as easy to see for those who are willing to see them as they are invisible to people who want to pretend they don't exist. Professor Mellor's suggestion that all horses be transitioned to pain-free bitless bridles (some bitless bridles are designed specifically to inflict pain) is not going to go down well in FEI sport. Like drugs, painful devices for control are seen as necessary to keep the show on the road. In fact, as of 2020, the FEI has banned the use of bitless bridles for the cross-country stage of eventing.

As the sport bleeds fans, the side-show becomes more and more undignified

All these problems have confounded the governing bodies of equestrian sport for decades. In 2015, the FEI began the task of re-vamping its image ahead of Rio 2016, to make Equestrian more broadly appealing. At times, the outlandishness of the promotional videos released by the FEI has been baffling. Human athletes performing human sports while wearing horse masks, all set in a 1980s universe with no actual horses appearing until the very end. Fun, but completely unrelated to FEI disciplines. Charlotte Dujardin in a turban—I still wonder what that was about. Animated discipline explainers featuring bitless horses, when—for years—the FEI has stubbornly rejected calls to include bitless riding at its dressage events. And who can forget Billy, the Rio 2016 FEI mascot? A heavily anthropomorphised horse, who was sick and tired of living at home in the countryside with his family, yearning instead for Olympic glory.

It is difficult to imagine how this content could possibly appeal to anyone seriously interested in horses or horse sport, but perhaps that is not its purpose. 'Internet popularity' now counts for such a significant chunk of a sport's classification for Olympic revenue share that, as long as the content generates interactions, it doesn't matter whether people think it is stupid or pointless. The people who like or share a video of a parkour virtuoso wearing a horse mask may have zero interest in FEI sport, but the interaction still shows up in the federation's digital statistics. Every click counts. In some ways, this approach is analogous to rollkur, de-nerving, and tight nosebands. It ignores the root cause of a serious problem, slaps on a bandaid to hide the symptoms, and keeps going as if everything is fine.

The FEI knows that its demographic is more interested in the horses themselves, and in the lifestyle which goes with riding them, than it is in the actual sport. At a broadcast and digital workshop put on for national federations by the FEI in 2018, managing director Peter Weber from research company IRIS showed participants a video clip of a small child trying to mount a Shetland pony.[6] The very homemade clip was entitled 'Never give up on your dreams.' At first, the girl was unsuccessful, but she persevered and eventually got on top of the pony. The clip had received 7.4

6 Peter Weber, 'The Market', presentation at the FEI NFs Broadcast & Digital Workshop, Lausanne, 31 Oct 2018, https://www.youtube.com/watch?v=h5Lw4bow02I, timecode 37:08, accessed 12 Sep 2021.

million clicks. For comparison, an expensively produced FEI video, full of action-packed equestrian sport, had received less than 200,000 clicks.

The two videos were apparently intended as a reminder that the most compelling content is not always that with the highest production cost, which is of course true. But this message also struck a chord with Charles Balchin, head of programming for IMG, the company which produces the content for the FEI’s streaming service, FEI TV. ‘Those two clips, in my opinion, sum up all the issues that we’re trying to resolve here’, Mr Balchin said, addressing workshop participants. ‘That little girl isn’t the sport, and that is the problem. How do we get the 7.4 million people who thought that was cute to actually want to watch the sport?’

The short answer to Mr Balchin’s question is, you don’t. This was perfectly—if perhaps unintentionally—summed up in an explanation given at the same digital marketing workshop by FEI Marketing Manager Vassilis Paradissis in his talk about branding:

> You have created your brand, you have created your beautiful image, you have created the idea of what you represent. You need to deliver. If our sport is exciting, beautiful, fair to the horse, your end product needs to deliver on all of these things because if not, basically, you do not have a brand.[7]

The FEI and its member federations cannot deliver. The sport is not exciting. At least not exciting enough, and due to the lowered qualification criteria to facilitate the increase in the number of flags at the Olympic Games, it has just become even less exciting. The sport is not beautiful—to anyone who dares to look, it is cruel and hideous. And it is not fair to the horse. How could it be, when it wastes horses’ bodies, their minds,

7 Vassilis Paradissis, ‘Brand and Brand Research’, presentation at the FEI NFs Broadcast & Digital Workshop, Lausanne, 31 Oct 2018, https://www.youtube.com/watch?v=MvMArHUqR4I, timecode 5:24, accessed 12 Sep 2021.

and the lives they could have lived for their own reasons? All the clever branding in the world cannot fix the fact that the product, as advertised, is not actually available for purchase. This is why 750 million people are apparently a little bit interested in horses, while horse sport struggles to be universally relevant.

11

Equestrian will not meet modern standards. Will the IOC?

Equestrian sport as practised at FEI events undoubtedly causes pain and distress to horses. As it is an unnecessary practice performed exclusively for human entertainment, it can be argued that it is against the law in several of the countries where the sport is most developed. The legal charges pressed against the IOC, the FEI, and individual riders following Tokyo 2020 are only the tip of the iceberg.

WHEN LUISE AND I FIRST started breaking stories about questionable riding at FEI competitions back in 2008, one reaction from industry insiders came consistently. People would ask us if we were trying to get the sport banned. Truly, we were not. We believed completely that it was possible to stage humane and ethically justifiable equestrian competitions, and we wanted the FEI to start doing that instead of what it was doing. It surprised and disappointed us that the people inside the sport didn't share our belief in it. To them, a choice had to be made between hiding the truth or waving goodbye to the sport. I have since learned that they were right and I was wrong. This is a sport that relies on the very practices it simultaneously labels as abuse, and has shown itself to be unable to improve. There are few better examples of that than the controversy surrounding the FEI's so-called blood rule.

Until 2018, the FEI Jumping Rules had a 'blood rule' by which any rider whose spurs drew blood was automatically disqualified for abuse of the horse. If you are not familiar with equestrian culture, you can be forgiven for assuming that this rule rested securely on a broad consensus. It did not.

Even Olympic riders injure their horses with their spurs. In the spring of 2016, the reigning Olympic jumping champion was disqualified at a 5* jumping event in Madrid for kicking his horse so hard with his spurs that he drew blood. As the horse, called Happiness, was approaching the water jump, she looked as if she was not going to make it. Her rider vigorously kicked her, and she ended up clearing the jump. 'That was well ridden', said one commentator on the livestream immediately, before elaborating on his compliment. 'A real exhibition of how to use your legs in an emergency.' Depending on their values, readers will have different views on which represents the greater emergency: incurring four faults in an FEI jumping competition, or punching a hole in a live animal. Seen through the eyes of an equestrian insider, this riding was excellent because it got the horse over the jump. To consider how getting kicked like that might feel for the horse most likely didn't even occur to the commentators, the rider or the stadium audience, because the kicking was considered 'necessary'.

Outside equestrian sport, many people would probably say that it was animal abuse to break the skin of a horse with a spur, in order to win a competition. Inside the sport, everyone knew that occasionally doing so was just part of the game. This meant that riders—even the best and most well thought of riders in the world—were regularly being disqualified and labelled as abusers for riding in a way which was considered correct and even admirable by their fellow insiders.

Horses are so commonly injured by the tools riders use to control them that equestrians become somewhat calloused to these incidents. Many riders felt that 'abuse' was too harsh a term for cutting their horse with a spur, and disqualification too harsh a sanction. One such rider was the USA's Georgina Bloomberg.

In July 2017, after her team-mate, Olympic gold medallist Scott Brash, was disqualified from a Global Champions League competition in Cascais, Ms Bloomberg wrote an open letter to the FEI, demanding a change to the blood rule. Referring to herself as 'the utmost animal lover', Ms Bloomberg candidly stated that injuring horses with spurs was unavoidable for professional riders, and demanded that the FEI change its rules to accommodate this fact:

> I understand that there are people who will state that no horse should ever have a mark or injury that was inflicted by its rider. Unfortunately, the reality that every horseman and woman knows is that the occasional injury or mark on a horse's skin is inevitable. Just as any athlete may experience a rub or bruise during play, a small spur mark on a horse's side is a consequence of high-level competition; it is not abuse. This is not a call to soften the rules on horse welfare, but simply to adjust the rules to be reasonable, fair and consistent.[1]

Ms Bloomberg did not stand alone. German Olympian Daniel Deusser told the *Chronicle of the Horse* in 2016 that he felt the blood rule destroyed the sport of jumping.[2] In the same article, several riders made similar statements. Nayal Nasser, an Olympic rider on the Egyptian team in Tokyo 2020, creatively suggested that, instead of automatic disqualification, stewards should make riders hide any minor spur marks:

---

1 Georgina Bloomberg, 'An Open Letter By Georgina Bloomberg', press release, 18 Jul 2017, Phelps Sports, https://phelpssports.com/open-letter-georgina-bloomberg/, accessed 22 Aug 2021.

2 Mollie Bailey, 'Taking A Tough Look At Blood', *Chronicle of the Horse*, 3 Oct 2016, https://www.chronofhorse.com/article/magazine-taking-tough-look-blood, accessed 22 Aug 2021.

> I understand [the FEI's] perspective. They don't want to see these kinds of things on TV. Now that the sport is getting so much mainstream attention that's the last thing that they want. The fix is easy: put a belly band on, and even if there is a rub on there no one will know.[3]

A belly band is a neoprene or elastic girdle which is officially used to avoid spur marks and unofficially used to hide them. Mr Nasser's suggestion might seem pragmatic, but the FEI obviously couldn't afford to write into its rules that officials, upon the discovery of something then classed as horse abuse, should refrain from sanctioning the rider and order them instead to hide the evidence. A subtler solution was required.

In recent years, the FEI has been forced by successive scandals into making a show of cracking down on cruelty in the sport. Even this small increase in steward vigilance has upset riders. As far as the riders are concerned, they are not abusing their horses, as long as they don't mean to be. Equestrian insiders will say things like: 'if I were hurting my horse, he wouldn't put up with it' or 'you can't force a 600-kilo animal to do something they don't want to do'. The industry is collectively in denial about the fact that the real world is turning its back on the gratuitous exploitation of even much larger and more dangerous animals, like orca and elephants; understanding that these animals, although large, can be forced to perform against their will, and often are.

In June 2021, the FEI suspended American Grand Prix rider Andrew Kocher for the use of electric spurs.[4] The devices, which the rider had rigged up himself by connecting a modified power bank to his metal spurs with wires running inside his clothes, had been used by Mr Kocher and several of his staff. The abuse went on for years at home and at

3 Bailey, 'Taking a Tough Look'.

4 FEI Tribunal, Decision in the matter of the FEI vs Andrew Kocher Reference-No. C20-0060, 10 Jun 2021, https://inside.fei.org/system/files/C20-0060_Final%20Decision_Mr%20Kocher%20HA02%20PDF.pdf, accessed 12 Sep 2021.

competitions, during which time Mr Kocher was very successful riding at top international level, and no FEI steward ever noticed he was using the illegal equipment. The matter only became known to the general public after someone tipped off the FEI's integrity unit and a French horse magazine. If horses could not be coerced to perform at elite level, stories like this would not exist. But they do.

Riders who have never questioned the premise of using animals for human entertainment just consider that they are doing whatever is necessary to achieve an end, for which the horse appears to them a natural means. Any pain or suffering inflicted on horses by riders for the purposes of winning is considered incidental. This forces the FEI into yet another balancing act between appeasing its riders and maintaining its social licence to operate, for which the sport depends on the acceptance of the general public.

Ms Bloomberg wrote her open letter to the FEI in July 2017. In November the same year, the FEI convened for its annual General Assembly. Among the proposed rule changes for jumping—sent out to stakeholders before the GA—was a softening of the blood rule, by which disqualification would no longer automatically result from the discovery that a rider had drawn blood with their spurs.[5]

Fear of litigation limits officials' ability to enforce the rules

Not only did the proposed rule changes downgrade spur wounds from abuse to casual mishap, but it also left it up to stewards to decide whether blood on a horse's sides would even result in elimination. 'Minor cases of blood on the flank(s) as described in the Jumping Stewards Manual do not incur elimination.'[6]

The International Jumping Officials Club (IJOC) did not like this

5 FEI, General Assembly Annex Pt. 15.3 bis, 17 Nov 2017, article 242, https://inside.fei.org/system/files/GA17_Annex_15.3_Bis_Published%20on%2027%20October_0.pdf, accessed 22 Aug 2021.

6 FEI, General Assembly Annex, article 241, 3.30.

proposal. Stewards are already caught between the liberties taken by entitled riders and a steward's duty on the frontlines to prevent yet more horse-abuse scandals from bringing on the implosion of the entire sport. In the notes to the proposed rule changes, the IJOC decried the lack of objectivity if the blood rule had to be applied on a case-by-case basis by its members. The IJOC also expressed concern that its members might be pressured or even sued by riders:

> Under the current rule and even in the clearest cases, the decision to disqualify an athlete is often hotly—not to mention publicly—contested. The proposed introduction of Art 241.3.30 and the change to the wording of Art 242.3.1 open the door for the athlete and his/her entourage to legitimately challenge any decision to eliminate or disqualify not only in situ and within the FEI legal system, but also to bring civil law suits against the officials who have taken those decisions.[7]

The officials had a point. Ms Bloomberg is the daughter of Michael Bloomberg, the former mayor of New York City and 2020 United States Presidential candidate. Someone like that could—if she wanted to—make life profoundly miserable for a lowly FEI steward. In her open letter to the FEI, Ms Bloomberg accused the FEI steward who discovered the blood on Mr Brash's horse in Cascais of having caused the bleeding themselves by 'harshly' rubbing the spur mark:

> As others watched, the steward rubbed the mark hard enough to make it bleed slightly, at which point, the steward took the glove to the foreign judge, who deferred to the president of the ground jury. After spreading a trace amount of blood across the horse's side, the steward photographed the cut, choosing to portray it in a manner that was not representative of how it looked when the horse originally exited the ring.[8]

7 FEI, General Assembly Annex, article 241, 3.30.

8 Bloomberg, 'An Open Letter'.

Like the gums of their horses, the egos of top riders are easily bruised, and it is a notoriously litigious demographic, so the officials couldn't be blamed for wanting to limit their subjective input to a minimum.

Conflicting views among member countries

There were other objections against the softening of the blood rule, besides that of the Officials Club. The Spanish Equestrian Federation pointed out the loss of objectivity, and called for the rules to be unchanged. President of the European Equestrian Federation, Dr Hanfried Haring, warned that changing the blood rule might damage the sport's image.

> Any softening of the current rule is extremely dangerous. On one hand we have to explain why we ask for performances of horses that apparently can only be achieved when accepting to inflict injury to a horse. On the other hand we need to ensure that stewards and judges are able to make comprehensible and consistent decisions.[9]

The German Equestrian Federation was partially against. It agreed to the downgrade of 'incidental' spur wounds from abuse to mistake, but it wanted riders to at least be eliminated in every case. To support its position, the German federation supplied a selection of comments it had received from the equestrian community in response to the proposal to soften the blood rule: 'profit prevails over animal welfare', 'it is all about the riders' greed no matter if the horse is doing well', 'a horse is not a piece of sports equipment', 'this would be a step back in horse welfare', 'horse sport is stuck somewhere in the 19th century', 'FEI loses its credibility—no wonder laymen think all of us riders are animal torturers', 'we may not look away'.[10]

9 FEI, General Assembly Annex, article 241, 3.30.

10 FEI, General Assembly Annex, p. 8.

The Norwegian Federation suggested that all international jumping riders should be limited to using pony spurs. Pony spurs are particularly short and blunt in order to protect ponies against inexperienced and impatient children who have not yet mastered the art of keeping their legs still on a horse in motion. The Norwegian Federation also warned against the effect on the sport's public image of easing the blood rule:

> Is it ever justifiable to puncture a horse's skin with a piece of equipment the athlete chooses to wear with the express intention of enhancing the performance of that horse, whether it was done intentionally or not? One could argue that the fact the athlete chooses to wear a spur that can puncture a horse's skin signifies intent.[11]

The Equestrian Federation of the Netherlands seemed mostly concerned with semantics. 'We believe that for the public opinion it would be better to use a friendlier word/description for "blood", as we use "banned medication" instead of "doping."'[12] Note here that not even the FEI's own member federations can understand its anti-doping rules well enough to use the correct terminology. There is no such thing as 'banned medication' in the FEI Equine Anti-Doping & Controlled Medications Regulations. Prohibited substances are either banned substances or controlled medications (or specified substances). The confusion is complete.

The Swiss Federation concurred with the Dutch federation about the word 'blood': '"Blood Rule" as mentioned in the eventing rules already sounds quite cruel.'[13] It does sound cruel, doesn't it? The Equestrian Federation of France also wanted a new name for the rule, '... in order to avoid extreme negative interpretations generated by the actual wording.' The general trend in the comments at the forum was

11 FEI, General Assembly Annex p. 9.

12 FEI, General Assembly Annex, p. 9.

13 FEI, General Assembly Annex, p. 9.

to express concern about the public image of the sport, not about the horses doing the bleeding.

As of 2018, the FEI has chosen to relegate the blood rule to chapter 241: Eliminations. This might seem like a minor change, but it was quite significant. Chapter 242 of the FEI Jumping Rules deals with various reasons for disqualification, including abuse of the horse. It was here that the blood rule originally resided. Chapter 241 deals with eliminations, which tend to result from the rider making a mistake, such as forgetting to jump an obstacle, falling off or being too slow. Furthermore, for a rider to be disqualified for excessive use of the spurs, an official (conscious of the possible rider blowback discussed above) now has to explicitly make that decision, even if the horse is bleeding from a spur wound. This solves a problem for the FEI, because it will bring down the number of cases of horse abuse in the sport, without effectively changing anything about how horses are treated. For instance, when it was discovered that New Zealand rider Daniel Meech had injured his mare, Cinca 3, with his spur during the individual jumping final at the Tokyo Olympic Games, it did not trigger news stories about horse abuse as similar cases had done in Rio. Rather than abuse, it was framed as a casual mishap. For the horse involved, the experience was no doubt unaltered by its re-branding.[14]

In the short run, the frequency of abuse *cases* will fall, due to the easing of the blood rule. The problem with this strategy is that spurs will continue to draw blood, photographers will continue to take pictures, and the general public will continue to dislike horses being made to bleed for human entertainment. Like rollkur and doping, it doesn't matter much to people outside the sport what the FEI chooses to call it. Insiders can

14 Eleanor Jones, '"She deserved her place": horse eliminated from individual Olympic showjumping under blood rule', *Horse & Hound*, 5 Aug 2021, https://www.horseandhound.co.uk/news/daniel-meech-olympics-757004, accessed 12 Sep 2021.

decry the 'ignorance of non-horsey people who just don't get that this is not abuse' from now until the cows come home. It won't help the sport's social licence to operate.

Equestrian may not meet modern legal codes

The entire blood rule discussion was about whether, once the horse gets to the stage where an injury from a spur actually bleeds, that can be called abuse, or whether that definition was too unfair on the riders. In the real world, abuse is not considered to be a question of whether or not the victim bleeds. Circus elephants don't have to bleed for people to support a ban on their exploitation. A video clip of a man kicking a dog will inspire rage and go viral, whether the dog bleeds or not. Horses suffer pain and anxiety from the use of spurs, long before they bleed—try poking yourself in the ribs with the unsharpened end of a pencil until you eventually break the skin, and you'll get the idea—and their injuries feel the same to them, whether humans frame them as 'abuse' or as 'bad luck'.

The obsessing over blood and semantics which takes place within the equestrian industry has little to do with animal ethics, and everything to do with keeping any abuse of FEI horses away from the public eye. The abuse itself will never be resolved or go away. It is intrinsic to the sport, and that means that the sport itself could in fact turn out to be illegal in countries where animals are protected by law against the infliction of unnecessary pain and distress, such as the UK, Sweden, Germany, Denmark, and—perhaps most salient to the IOC—Switzerland. It is only a matter of time before these countries begin to enforce their legislation in ways which limit the practice of equestrian sport. How will France deal with hosting the Olympic Games in 2024, considering that administering drugs to horses is illegal there, if it happens for the purpose of making them able or better able to participate in sporting events?

Back in 2010, FEI General Counsel Lisa Lazarus explained this to delegates at the NSAIDs conference: 'French law clearly prohibits the administration of NSAIDs during or in order to take part in competition. Offences can be sanctioned by criminal law and administrative law.'[15]

FEI Clean Sport operates with an unnecessarily generous threshold for aspirin, and treating veterinarians can ask the FEI for permission to treat horses during events with other prohibited substances as well, including various NSAIDs, local anaesthetics, diuretics and sedatives.

It will be interesting to see, at the Games of the XXXIII Olympiad, whether French law or FEI rules and regulations will apply, because the two are not compatible. Will every request for permission to drug horses with NSAIDs and other drugs that mask symptoms of injury be declined at the Paris Olympic Games as they should be according to French law? Will Olympic athletes who have already medicated their horses before submitting their veterinary forms be reported to the police? How is it all going to work?

The blue tongue photos we published in 2014 might have resulted in a conviction for animal cruelty, had the rider—an Olympic medallist—not backtracked in court and denied what he had previously admitted in a magazine interview: that the tongue was blue and the fault was his. More such cases will follow. Right now, all eyes are on the criminal cases against the German pentathlete and her coach, the FEI and the IOC for horse abuse at the Olympic Games.

Public exposure of abuse will only increase

The truth about blue tongues and other equestrian atrocities is that they aren't rare. They can just be a bit tricky to document. If the right

15 Lisa Lazarus, 'A Pan-European Overview of National Laws On The Use of NSAIDs in Equestrian Competition', FEI NSAID Congress, YouTube video, 29 Aug 2012, timecode: 12:48, https://www.youtube.com/watch?v=Rh91MJi7vDk&t=1391s, accessed 22 Aug 2021.

photographer can get close enough to the competition, they can take a lot of horrific photos, including depictions of rollkur, blue tongues and bleeding spur wounds. The FEI relies on the photographers it accredits to have the good manners to throw away any incriminating photos and stick to publishing the pretty ones. However, the future of sports broadcasting includes previously unimaginable image quality, interactivity, the ability to watch in virtual reality, and ultra-high-speed replays. Anybody will be able to document a blue tongue, a spur wound or a horse with a 'joker smile'—the corners of the lips ripped open by the rider's violent pulling on the reins. Riders will be incriminating themselves on live television—almost definitely from the arena of the Olympic Games.

I watched every single equestrian event from Tokyo. Not because I wanted to. I am one of the people who can't watch anymore. But I made myself do it because I wanted to see how dire things have become and how easy it was to document without even being at the event. I took hundreds of screenshots. Each of them hideous enough to prompt cries of disgust from my otherwise fairly jaded network. Even the FEI's own beauty shots, shared on Instagram to strike its followers with awe, were ugly enough that a medium sized international shitstorm could have been effortlessly stirred if we had shared them on our own social media with the 70,000 ex-fans of Equestrian who follow us there.

The years of inaction by the FEI and its national federations has enabled the ugly, violent riding to become so normalised that I can now sit in my living room and take pictures at least as grotesque as the ones we used to have to hang out backstage to get.

Because of social media, stories of top riders misusing horses spread too fast for effective damage control. In July 2020, video footage was leaked of Brazilian Olympic dressage rider and shortlisted Tokyo 2020 hopeful Leandro Da Silva—a full sized adult man—riding a tiny Shetland pony whom he was beating and punishing harshly by way of yanking on the reins. Footage also emerged of the rider's adult son, forcing the pony to carry him over jumps and causing a dangerous, rotational fall, whereby the pony landed on his back. The most astonishing thing about these videos is that they became public because the rider's son could not resist sharing them with friends, believing them to be hilarious. Laughing can be heard in both video clips as well as the young videographer suggesting that the pony, called Pirulito, is his father's next Olympic mount.[16] As you will no doubt have realised by now, such callousness is no rarity in FEI sport. Stories like this will keep coming because behaviour like this is commonplace. The FEI can do nothing except sacrifice the occasional rider for good measure whenever a media storm arises. Mr Da Silva received a three-year ban for his behaviour. He will be eligible to compete again in time for the Paris Olympiad in 2024.

Over to you, IOC

The younger generations, to whom you seek to impart Olympic values, are flocking to social justice issues, including non-human animal rights. They are giving up cheese because they don't want to rob a calf of his mother. They are giving up eggs because they care about the reproductive health of hens. Going to Sea World is no longer cool. How are you going to sell these young idealists the performance of horses who are being forced to participate, who live their entire lives in crates, and who are made to spend hours and hours every week trying to balance on the back of a truck with their heads tied to the wall? Horses who are spurred until they bleed, who have their mouths strapped shut, their tongues crushed, their lips torn, and whose trauma and social deprivation render them physically ill and mentally unbalanced? All for human entertainment.

16 Pippa Cuckson, 'Dressage Olympian Banned Three Years for Abusing Daughter's Pony', Horsesport, 21 April 2021, https://horsesport.com/horse-news/dressage-olympian-banned-three-years-abusing-daughters-pony/, accessed 22 Aug 2021.

Credibility, sustainability, youth. The three pillars of your Olympic Agenda 2020. Why don't you walk the walk as well as talk the talk? Young people say they want an inhabitable planet and a fair world. They are watching their carbon footprint and minimising their air travel for the greater good of humanity. How are you going to sell them the idea of flying horses back and forth between continents every few months so that they can win money for people who are already rich? You can't, and neither can the FEI. Sooner or later, you will discontinue Equestrian. It is only a question of when. Now you have all the arguments you need. Now you know. This manuscript is evidence that you've been told. What you do next is up to you.

Bibliography

Ankerdal, Steen, 'VM-ryttere bruger dopinglæge', *B.T.*, 29 Jul 2002.

Appels, Astrid, 'Two Months Suspension for Ulla Salzgeber', Eurodressage, 6 Feb 2004, https://www.eurodressage.com/2004/02/06/two-months-suspension-ulla-salzgeber, accessed 20 Aug 2021.

Appels, Astrid, 'Andreas Helgstrand Back in the Hot Seat after Publication Falsterbo Training Photos', Eurodressage, 27 Aug 2015, https://www.eurodressage.com/2015/08/27/andreas-helgstrand-back-hot-seat-after-publication-falsterbo-training-photos, accessed 22 Aug 2021.

Appels, Astrid, 'Anky van Grunsven Sues Eurodressage', Eurodressage, 25 Aug 2010, https://www.eurodressage.com/2010/08/25/anky-van-grunsven-sues-eurodressage, accessed 22 Aug 2021.

Appels, Astrid, 'FEI Judges Not Permitted to Judge Online Dressage Competitions', Eurodressage, 15 Apr 2020, https://www.eurodressage.com/2020/04/15/fei-judges-not-permitted-judge-online-dressage-competitions, accessed 19 Aug 2021.

Appels, Astrid, 'Sjef Janssen, Dr. Rene van Weeren and Anky van Grunsven on Coaching and Hyperflexion', Eurodressage, 6 Nov 2006, https://www.eurodressage.com/2006/11/06/sjef-janssen-dr-rene-van-weeren-and-anky-van-grunsven-coaching-and-hyperflexion, accessed 3 Oct 2021.

Bailey, Mollie, 'Taking A Tough Look At Blood', *Chronicle of the Horse*, 3 Oct 2016, https://www.chronofhorse.com/article/magazine-taking-tough-look-blood, accessed 22 Aug 2021.

Bakalus, Silla, 'OL-rytter i Lønskandale', *B.T.*, 12 Aug 2013, https://www.bt.dk/danmark/ol-rytter-i-loenskandale, accessed 22 Aug 2021.

Bakalus, Silla, 'Nye anklager mod toprytter: Ville snyde for millioner', *B.T.*, 11 May 2014, https://www.bt.dk/krimi/nye-anklager-mod-toprytter-ville-snyde-for-millioner, accessed 22 Aug 2021.

Bankes, Caroline, 'Half of all sport horses are lame, study finds', *Horse & Hound*, 28 April 2014, https://www.horseandhound.co.uk/news/half-horses-lame-saddle-slip-survey-428728, accessed 21 Aug 2021.

Bell, Catherine, Suzanne Rogers, Julie Taylor and Debbie Busby, 'Improving the Recognition of Equine Affective States', *Animals* 9/12 (2019), https://www.researchgate.net/publication/337941121_Improving_the_Recognition_of_Equine_Affective_States, accessed Aug 2021. doi: 10.3390/ani9121124

Bergmann, Iris, 'Naturalness and the Legitimacy of Thoroughbred Racing: A Photo-Elicitation Study with Industry and Animal Advocacy Informants', *Animals*, 10/9 (2020), https://www.researchgate.net/publication/343926314_Naturalness_and_the_Legitimacy_of_Thoroughbred_Racing_A_Photo-Elicitation_Study_with_Industry_and_Animal_Advocacy_Informants, accessed 7 Sep 2021. doi: 10.3390/ani10091513

Bloomberg, Georgina, 'An Open Letter By Georgina Bloomberg', press release, 18 Jul 2017, Phelps Sports, https://phelpssports.com/open-letter-georgina-bloomberg/, accessed 22 Aug 2021.

Boone, J Allen, *Kinship With All Life*, (San Francisco, Harper, 1954), p. 47.

Buntenkötter, Kathrin, 'Pharmacokinetics and in vitro efficacy of salicylic acid after oral administration of acetylsalicylic acid in horses', *BMC Veterinary Research*, 13/28 (2016), https://www.ncbi.nlm.nih.gov/pmc/articles/PMC5247822/, accessed 20 Aug 2021. doi: 10.1186/s12917-017-0955-1

Carlskov, Thor, 'Olympiske magtmænd truer danske journalister', *Ekstra Bladet*, 14 Aug 2012, https://ekstrabladet.dk/sport/anden_sport/anden_sport/article4016413.ece, accessed 22 Aug 2021.

Christensen, Nynne Bjerre, 'Forbund i opløsning efter magtkamp og dopingskandale', *Berlingske Tidende*, 23 Jun 2002.

Christensen, Nynne Bjherre and Lars Werge Andersen, 'Vennernes Forbund', *Berlingske Tidende*, 25 Jan 1998.

Clarkson, Neil, 'The drugs vote that rained on the FEI's parade', HorseTalk, 17 Dec 2009, https://www.horsetalk.co.nz/features/feihorsedoping-174.shtml, accessed 20 Aug 2021.

Court of Arbitration for Sport, CAS 2008/A/1700 Deutsche Reiterliche Vereinigung e. V. v/FEI & Christian Ahlmann CAS 2008/A/1710 Christian Ahlmann v/FEI, 30 Apr 2009, https://arbitrationlaw.com/sites/default/files/free_pdfs/CAS%202008-A-1700%20DRV%20v%20FEI%20%26%20CA%20%26%20CAS%202008-A-1710%20CA%20v%20FEI%20Award.pdf, accessed 20 Aug 2021.

Court of Arbitration for Sport, CAS 2012/A/2808 Abdullah Waleed Sharbatly v. Fédération Équestre Internationale, 17 Jul 2021, https://inside.fei.org/system/files/LOBSTER%20-%20CAS%20Final%20Decision%20-%2017%20July%202012.pdf, accessed 20 Aug 2021.

Cuckson, Pippa, 'Shocking Vote Legalizes Bute In FEI Competition,' *Chronicle of the Horse*, 20 Nov 2009, https://www.chronofhorse.com/article/shocking-vote-legalizes-bute-fei-competition, accessed 20 Aug 2021.

Cuckson, Pippa, 'Dressage Olympian Banned Three Years for Abusing Daughter's Pony', Horsesport.com, 21 April 2021, https://horsesport.com/horse-news/dressage-olympian-banned-three-years-abusing-daughters-pony/, accessed 22 Aug 2021.

Dansk Ride Forbunds Disciplinærudvalg, *Kendelse i sag om udelukkelse af hest fra fremtidig deltagelse i konkurrencer*, PDF downloaded from Danish Equestrian Federation website on 17 Jun 2017.

Decarpentry, General Albert, *Academic Equitation,* 1988 edition tr. Nicole Bartle, (London, J.A. Allen, 1949).

Deutscher Tierschutzbund, 'Deutscher Tierschutzbund erstattet Anzeige gegen Fünfkämpferin Annika Schleu und ihre Trainerin' (The German Animal Welfare Federation files criminal charges against pentathlete Annika Schleu and her trainer), 13 August 2021, https://www.tierschutzbund.de/news-storage/heimtiere/130821-pferdemisshandlung-bei-olympia-deutscher-tierschutzbund-stellt-strafanzeige-gegen-trainerin-und-reiterin, accessed 4 Sep 2021.

Doherty, Orla, Vincent Casey, Paul McGreevy, and Sean Arkins, 'Noseband Use in Equestrian Sports - An International Study'. *PLoS One*, 12/1 (2017)e0169060, https://pubmed.ncbi.nlm.nih.gov/28045961/. doi:10.1371/journal.pone.0169060

Epona TV, 'Blue Tongue World Cup', YouTube video, 20 Oct 2009, https://www.youtube.com/watch?v=8hIXGiV4N4k.

Epona TV, 'Anky van Grunsven Talks About her Method', YouTube video, 26 Oct 2009, https://www.youtube.com/watch?v=svOBsSdjUvU.

Epona TV, 'FEI Officials at Work', YouTube video, 28 June 2011, https://www.youtube.com/watch?v=n99uFM4XCs8.

European US Asian Equine Lawyers, 'Mathilda Karlsson's successful appeal to the CAS against the FEI', 20 May 2021, https://www.europeanequinelawyers.com/mathilda-karlssons-successful-appeal-to-the-cas-against-the-fei/, accessed 12 Sep 2021.

Eventing Nation, '#MeToo: A Letter to Myself as a Young Rider', 15

Dec 2017, https://eventingnation.com/metoo-a-letter-to-myself-as-a-young-rider/, accessed 19 Aug 2021.

FEI, 'A mile in their shoes', press release, 9 Nov 2016, https://www.fei.org/stories/a-mile-in-their-shoes, accessed 18 Aug 2021.

FEI, 'An Audit into Eventing Incorporating an Analysis of Risk Factors for Cross Country Horse Falls at FEI Eventing Competitions', 26 July 2016, https://inside.fei.org/system/files/Eventing%20Audit%20-%20Charles%20Barnett%20-%20Final%20Report%2026.07.16.pdf, accessed 22 Aug 2021.

FEI, Decision in the Positive Medication Case involving the horse MYTHILUS, 21 Sep 2008, https://inside.fei.org/media-updates/decision-positive-medication-case-involving-horse-mythilus, accessed 20 Aug 2021.

FEI, 'Dressage Future', Sports Forum Session 3 presentation, 27-28 Apr 2015, https://inside.fei.org/system/files/DRE%20Future_Session%203.pdf, accessed 21 Aug 2021.

FEI, Dressage Rules 2021, https://inside.fei.org/sites/default/files/FEI_Dressage_Rules_2021_Clean_Version_0.pdf, accessed 21 Aug 2021.

FEI, 'Equestrian Snapshots—Haitian Equestrian Federation' YouTube video, 24 Mar 2015, https://www.youtube.com/watch?v=F8ymfI661OU&feature=emb_title, accessed 19 Aug 2021.

FEI, Eventing Rules, 25th edition, https://inside.fei.org/sites/default/files/Eventing%20Rules%20for%202021%20-%20clean%20version%20-%2010.12.2020_0.pdf, accessed 21 Aug 2021.

FEI, Facebook post, 5 Aug 2012, https://www.facebook.com/the.fei/posts/402040016510063?comment_id=402103173170414, accessed 22 Aug 2021.

FEI, 'FEI General Assembly: Task Force on Anti Doping and Medication Policy', 9 Apr 2005, https://inside.fei.org/media-updates/fei-general-assembly-task-force-anti-doping-and-

medication-policy, accessed 20 Aug 2021.
FEI, 'FEI General Assembly Votes for New Anti-Doping Measures', press release, 19 Nov 2009, https://dressage-news.com/2009/11/19/fei-general-assembly-votes-for-new-ant-doping-measures, accessed 20 Aug 2021.
FEI, 'FEI Permitted Treating Veterinarians', https://data.fei.org/OffListRpts/OfficialsByAddRole_TV.pdf, accessed 20 Aug 2021.
FEI, 'FEI Reining Committee agrees new rule structure', media update, 1 Aug 2011, https://inside.fei.org/media-updates/fei-reining-committee-agrees-new-rules-structure, accessed 4 Oct 2021.
FEI, 'FEI Round-Table Conference Resolves Rollkur Controversy', media update, 8 Feb 2010, https://inside.fei.org/media-updates/fei-round-table-conference-resolves-rollkur-controversy, accessed 21 Aug 2021.
FEI, Financial Charges for the year 2021, 23 Nov 2020, https://inside.fei.org/system/files/2021%20Financial%20Charges.pdf, accessed 19 Aug 2021.
FEI, General Assembly Annex, https://inside.fei.org/system/files/GA17_Annex_15.3_Bis_Published%20on%2027%20October_0.pdf, accessed 22 Aug 2021.
FEI General Assembly in Moscow, YouTube video, 19 Nov 2019. https://www.youtube.com/watch?v=XEXWqq1XbNI&t=2108s, accessed 18 Aug 2021.
FEI, General Regulations, 1 Jan 2021, https://inside.fei.org/sites/default/files/FEI%20General%20Regulations-effective-1Jan2021-27Nov2020-Final-Clean.pdf, accessed 19 Aug 2021.
FEI, 'How Equestrianism is Bringing Hope to Haiti', 27 Feb 2018, https://www.fei.org/stories/lifestyle/horse-human/equestrianism-haiti-hope, accessed 19 Aug 2021.
FEI, information sheet, 2019, https://inside.fei.org/system/files/

Introducing_the_FEI_continous_2019.pdf, accessed 18 Aug 2021.

FEI, 'It's time for Africa', 29 Nov 2018, https://www.fei.org/stories/lifestyle/horse-human/africa-equestrian-solidarity, accessed 4 Sep 2021.

FEI, Jumping Rules, 25th edition, https://inside.fei.org/sites/default/files/Jumping_Rules_2021_clean.pdf, accessed 21 Aug 2021.

FEI, National Federations database, https://data.fei.org/NFPages/NF/Search.

FEI, NSAID Congress Question and Answer Session, YouTube video published 1 Sep 2010, https://www.youtube.com/watch?v=kCP707F70Vc&t=2923s, accessed 20 Aug 2021.

FEI, 'Olympic equestrian #TwoHearts campaign captures hearts around the world', press release, 17 May 2016, https://inside.fei.org/media-updates/olympic-equestrian-twohearts-campaign-captures-hearts-around-world, accessed 19 Aug 2021.

FEI, 'Report of the FEI Veterinary and Dressage Committees' Workshop: The use of over bending ("Rollkur") in FEI Competition', 31 Jan 2006 (Updated and revised version published 5 Mar 2006), no longer available online.

FEI, 'Report of the statutory auditor to the General Assembly on the financial statements', 2019, https://inside.fei.org/fei/about-fei/publications/fei-annual-report/2019/wp-content/uploads/2020/05/FEI-ROR-2019-with-2-signatures.pdf, accessed 19 Aug 2021.

FEI, 'The FEI absolutely condemns all cruel or aggressive training methods', Facebook post, 5 Aug 2012, https://www.facebook.com/the.fei/posts/402040016510063?comment_id=402103173170414, accessed 22 Aug 2021.

FEI, The FEI Solidarity Programme—FEI Course for NFs Secretaries General & Administrators, Lausanne (SUI)

October 2019, https://zanef.com/app/uploads/2019/11/FEI-Services-Tools-FEI-Solidarity-Programme-2019.pdf.

FEI, 'The Horse as a "Happy Athlete"', 4 Dec 2004, https://inside.fei.org/media-updates/2004-global-dressage-forum, accessed 21 Aug 2021.

FEI, Veterinary Regulations, 12th edition, 2010, https://equestrianorganizers.com/uploads_nieuws/documenten/2009-12-21-11:56:12_FEI%20Veterinary%20Regulations%2012th%20edition-in%20force%20on%205April10.pdf, accessed 20 Aug 2021.

FEI, 2014 Veterinary Regulations, 13th edition, 1 Jan 2014, https://www.dierenkliniekecht.nl/sites/default/files/documenten/FEI_Veterinary_Regulations_2014.pdf, accessed 21 Aug 2021.

FEI 'Workshop in Lausanne', media update, 31 Jan 2006, https://inside.fei.org/media-updates/fei-workshop-lausanne, accessed 21 Aug 2021.

FEI Tribunal, Decision of the FEI Tribunal, Case: 2019/CM04, 22 Apr 2020, https://inside.fei.org/system/files/Case_2019-CM04-LOBITA-Final_Tribunal_Decision-Approval_of_Agreement_between_Parties-22_April_2020.pdf, accessed 20 Aug 2021.

FEI Tribunal, Decision of the FEI Tribunal: Case number: FEI 2020/BS07 – EASY BOY 23, 7 Apr 2021, https://inside.fei.org/system/files/20210407_Final%20Decision%202020-BS07%20EASY%20BOY%2023%20-%20C21-0011%20-%20ALBISU.pdf, accessed 5 Sep 2021.

FEI Tribunal, Decision of the FEI Tribunal: Case number: FEI 2020/BS04 – GUCCI, 25 Jan 2021. https://inside.fei.org/system/files/20210125_Final%20Decision%20C21-0002%20-%20%202020%20BS04%20GUCCI.pdf, accessed 5 Sep 2021.

FEI Tribunal, Decision in the matter of the FEI vs Andrew Kocher Reference-No. C20-0060, 10 Jun 2021, https://inside.fei.org/

system/files/C20-0060_Final%20Decision_Mr%20Kocher%20 HA02%20PDF.pdf, accessed 12 Sep 2021.

Friend, Nick, 'From the horse's mouth: Ralph Straus on the commercial growth of equestrian's seven disciplines', SportsPro, 11 Oct 2018, https://www.sportspromedia.com/from-the-magazine/fei-equestrian-ralph-straus-commercial, accessed 22 Aug 2021.

Gaughan, Earl, 'Pain Recognition and Management in Horses', Merck Animal Health, 2018, https://www.merck-animal-health-equine.com/news/article/34, accessed 20 Aug 2021.

Gibson, Owen 'Danny Boyle urged to drop live animals from Olympics opening ceremony', *The Guardian*, 22 Jun 2012, https://www.theguardian.com/sport/2012/jun/22/danny -boyle-animals-olympics, accessed 19 Aug 2021.

Gorecka-Bruzda, Aleksandra, 'Conflict behaviour in elite show jumping and dressage horses', *Journal of Veterinary Behaviour Clinical Applications and Research*, 10/2 (2014), https://www.researchgate.net/publication/271226102_Conflict_behavior_in_elite_show_jumping_and_dressage_horses, accessed 19 Aug 2021. doi:10.1016/j.jveb.2014.10.004

Gutierrez-Nibeyro, Santiago, N.M. Werpy, Nathaniel White, M.A .Mitchell, R.B. Edwards, R.D. Mitchell, S. Gold, and A.K. Allen, 'Outcome of palmar/plantar digital neurectomy in horses with foot pain evaluated with magnetic resonance imaging: 50 cases (2005-2011)', *Equine Veterinary Journal.* 47/2 (2014), https://www.researchgate.net/publication/260678528_Outcome_of_palmarplantar_digital_neurectomy_in_horses_with_foot_pain_evaluated_with_magnetic_resonance_imaging_50_cases_2005-2011, accessed 5 Sep 2021. doi: 10.1111/evj.12262

Heiniger, Sandro and Hugues Mercier, 'Judging the Judges: A General Framework for Evaluating the Performance of International Sports Judges', https://arxiv.org/pdf/1807.10055.pdf, accessed 21

Aug 2021.

HorseTalk staff writer, 'Repeated studies show shortcomings among riders in identifying lameness in horses', HorseTalk, 26 Mar 2017, https://www.horsetalk.co.nz/2017/03/26/shortcomings -riders-lameness-horses/#axzz4cc0EeQhE, accessed 20 Aug 2021.

Houge, Knut, 'Han punkterte advokatens forsvarstale', Hest Norge, 28 Jun 2010, https://www.hest.no/article.html?news.nid=5129, accessed 20 Aug 2021.

International Jumping Riders Club, Video stream of panel debate during General Assembly, 22 Aug 2019, Facebook video, https://www.facebook.com/137022876422544/videos/ 1198035320378569, accessed 18 Aug 2021.

International Olympic Committee (IOC), Olympic Charter, 17 July 2020, https://olympics.com/ioc/olympic-charter.

International Society for Equitation Science, 'Position statement on restrictive nosebands', 2019, https://equitationscience.com/ equitation/position-statement-on-restrictive-nosebands, accessed 21 Aug 2021.

Jeffcott, Leo, 'FEI position on anti-doping in equestrian sport', presentation at the University of Sydney, 2005, slide 28/59, https://slideplayer.com/slide/3453820/, accessed 20 Aug 2021.

Jeffcott, Leo and colleagues, 'Letter from FEI Vets to Princess Haya Against Bute', Eventing Nation, Nov 2009, https://eventingnation. com/letter-from-fei-vets-against-fei-ruling/, accessed 20 Aug 2021.

Jones, Eleanor, '"She deserved her place": horse eliminated from individual Olympic showjumping under blood rule', *Horse & Hound*, 5 Aug 2021, https://www.horseandhound.co.uk/news/ daniel-meech-olympics-757004, accessed 12 Sep 2021.

Jurga, Fran, 'Rollkur Revolt: FEI Makes Official Statement Discouraging Overflexion in Dressage Training', Equus Magazine, 18

Apr 2008, https://equusmagazine.com/blog-equus/rollkur-revolt-fei-makes-official-statement-discouraging-overflexion-in-dressage-training, accessed 21 Aug 2021.

Jurga, Fran, 'Olympic Drug Tests: Add Pessoa to Offenders List', *Equus* magazine, 1 Sep 2008, https://equusmagazine.com/blog-equus/olympic-drug-tests-add-pessoa-to-offenders-list, accessed 20 Aug 2021.

Koch, Ludwig, *Die Reitkunst im Bilde*, (Hildesheim, 1998) [first published 1928], https://books.google.dk/books?id=t698Mn_GX7AC&printsec=frontcover&hl=da&source=gbs_ge_summary_r&cad=0#v=onepage&q&f=false, accessed 21 Aug 2021.

Lashley, Morgan J.J.O., Sandra Nauwelaerts, J.C.M. Vernooij, W. Back, and Hilary M. Clayton, 'Comparison of the head and neck position of elite dressage horses during top-level competitions in 1992 versus 2008', *The Veterinary Journal*, 202/3, (2014), https://www.sciencedirect.com/science/article/abs/pii/S1090023314003657, accessed 21 Aug 2021. doi: 10.1016/j.tvjl.2014.08.028

Lazarus, Lisa 'A Pan-European Overview of National Laws On The Use of NSAIDs in Equestrian Competition', FEI NSAID Congress, YouTube video, 29 Aug 2012, https://www.youtube.com/watch?v=Rh91MJi7vDk&t=1391s, accessed 22 Aug 2021.

Legacy for Animals, 'What We Request' (open letter to the Governor of Tokyo and the Tokyo Organising Committee of the Olympic and Paralympic Games), Aug 2018, https://legacyforanimals.com/en/tag/dotsie-bausch/, accessed 19 Aug 2021.

Melissen, Jacob, 'Dutch Vet – Jan Greve – An explosive interview', *The Horse* Magazine, 23 Feb 2018, https://www.horsemagazine.com/thm/2018/02/dutch-vet-jan-greve-an-explosive-interview/, accessed 20 Aug 2021.

Mellor, David J., 'Mouth Pain in Horses: Physiological Foundations, Behavioural Indices, Welfare Implications, and a Suggested Solution', *Animals*, 10/4 (2020), https://doi.org/10.3390/ani10040572.

Mellor, David J., Ngaio J Beausoleil, Katharine E Littlewood, Andrew N McLean, Paul D. McGreevy, Bidda Jones and Christina Wilkins, 'The 2020 Five Domains Model: Including Human–Animal Interactions in Assessment of Animal Welfare', *Animals* 10/10 (2020), https://doi.org/10:3390/ani10101870.

Murray, R.C., S.J. Dyson, C. Tranquille and V. Adams, 'Association of type of sport and performance level with anatomical site of orthopaedic injury diagnosis', *Equine Exercise Physiology* 7, *Equine vet. J., suppl.* 36 (2006), https://beva.onlinelibrary.wiley.com/doi/pdfdirect/10.1111/j.2042-3306.2006.tb05578.x, accessed 21 Aug 2021.

Nir, Sarah Maslin, 'Whispers of Sexual Abuse Tailed an Equestrian Legend for Decades. At 81, He Was Barred for Life', *New York Times*, 8 Aug 2019, https://www.nytimes.com/2019/08/08/sports/george-morris.html, accessed 19 Aug 2021

Nir, Sarah Maslin, 'The Equestrian Coach Who Minted Olympians, and Left a Trail of Child Molestation', *New York Times*, 29 May 2019, https://www.nytimes.com/2018/05/29/sports/jimmy-williams-flintridge.html?module=inline, accessed 19 Aug 2021.

Nørgaard, Malte, 'Dansk dressurstjerne fik kæmpebøde for ulovlig arbejdskraft', *DR*, 18 Jan 2008, https://www.dr.dk/sporten/oevrig/dansk-dressurstjerne-fik-kaempeboede-ulovlig-arbejdskraft, accessed 22 Aug 2021.

Owers, Roly, 'A social license for equestrian sport', YouTube video of talk at FEI regional meeting, 29 Apr 2020, https://www.youtube.com/watch?v=OtWcN1N13TQ&t=12s, timecode 48:00, accessed 19 Aug 2021.

Paradissis, Vassilis, 'Brand and Brand Research', presentation at the FEI NFs Broadcast & Digital Workshop, Lausanne, 31 Oct 2018, https://www.youtube.com/watch?v=MvMArHUqR4I, accessed 12 Sep 2021.

Pérez-Manrique, Lucia, Karina León-Pérez, Emmanuel Zamora-Sánchez, Sarah Davies, Christopher Ober, Bethany Wilson, and Paul McGreevy, 'Prevalence and Distribution of Lesions in the Nasal Bones and Mandibles of a Sample of 144 Riding Horses', *Animals* 10/9 (2020), 1661. https://doi.org/10.3390/ani10091661.

Phillips, Carol, 'Carl Hester "appalled" by sale of Uthopia by auction', *Horse & Hound*, 28 April 2016, https://www.horseandhound.co.uk/news/carl-hester-appalled-sale-uthopia-auction-533937, accessed 4 Sep 2021.

Reiche, Danyel, *Success and Failure of Countries at the Olympic Games* (New York, Routledge, 2016).

Reuters, 'Amazon jaguar shot dead after Olympic torch ceremony', 21 Jun 2016, https://www.reuters.com/article/olympics-rio-jaguar-idUKL8N19D5AY, accessed 19 Aug 2021.

St. Georg staff, 'Dressur Pervers', *St. Georg*, Jul 2005, https://www.st-georg.de/hintergrund/rollkur/dressur-pervers-aus-st-georg-juli2005/, accessed 21 Aug 2021.

Simeoni, Evi, 'Reiterliche Vereinigung suspendiert Beerbaum', *Frankfurter Allgemeine*, 28 May 2009, https://www.faz.net/aktuell/sport/mehr-sport/alle-spitzenkader-aufgeloest-reiterliche-vereinigung-suspendiert-beerbaum-1802635.html, accessed 20 Aug 2021.

Stauffer, Caroline, 'Equestrian: Four show jumpers disqualified by "blood rule"', Reuters, 17 Aug 2016, https://www.reuters.com/article/us-olympics-rio-equestrian-jumpingteam-b-idUSKCN10S27Y, accessed 12 Sep 2021.

Tomlinson, Laura, 'Olympic judges, please mark what you see, not who you see', *Horse & Hound*, 20 July 2021, https://www.horseandhound.co.uk/plus/opinion/laura-tomlinson-olympic-judges-marking-753444, accessed 21 Aug 2021.

Uldahl, M. and H.M. Clayton, 'Lesions associated with the use of bits, nosebands, spurs and whips in Danish competition horses', *Equine Veterinary Journal*, 51/2 (2019), https://doi.org/10.1111/evj.12827.

Weber, Peter, 'The Market', presentation at the FEI NFs Broadcast & Digital Workshop, Lausanne, 31 Oct 2018, https://www.youtube.com/watch?v=h5Lw4bow02I, accessed 12 Sep 2021.

Wild beim Wild, 'Strafanzeige gegen IOC und FEI', 16 Aug 2021, https://wildbeimwild.com/kampagnen/strafanzeige-gegen-ioc-und-fei/49553/2021/08/16/, accessed 22 Aug 2021.

Willis, Grania, 'Equestrian world shocked by schizophrenia drug allegations', *The Irish Times*, 3 Nov 2004, https://www.irishtimes.com/news/equestrian-world-shocked-by-schizophrenia-drug-allegations-1.1164686, accessed 20 Aug 2021.

ZANEF Financial Report 2016, https://zanef.com/app/uploads/2017/01/AGM-2017-08-2016-Financial-Report.pdf, accessed 18 Aug 2021.

ZANEF Financial Report 2017, https://zanef.com/app/uploads/2018/02/AGM-2018-07-Financial-Report-2017-Budget-2018.pdf, accessed 19 Aug 2021.

ZANEF Financial Report 2018, https://zanef.com/app/uploads/2019/02/ZANEF-Accounts-2018-FOR-CIRCULARIZATIONxls-1.pdf, accessed 19 Aug 2021.

ZANEF, Solidarity Coach recon document, 2017 ZANEF AGM, https://zanef.com/app/uploads/2017/01/ZANEF-AGM-2017-21-AGM-Solidarity-Coach-Recon-.pdf, accessed 19 Aug 2021.

CPSIA information can be obtained
at www.ICGtesting.com
Printed in the USA
LVHW111058250122
709338LV00006B/96

9 788797 354308